To READ Stuff You Have To KNOW Stuff

Books by Kelly Gallagher

Reading Reasons

Deeper Reading

Teaching Adolescent Writers

Readicide

Write Like This

In the Best Interest of Students

180 Days
with Penny Kittle

4 Essential Studies
with Penny Kittle

To Read Stuff You Have to Know Stuff

Kelly Gallagher

To READ Stuff You Have To KNOW Stuff

Helping Students Build and Use **Prior Knowledge**

HEINEMANN • **Portsmouth, NH**

Heinemann
145 Maplewood Avenue, Suite 300
Portsmouth, NH 03801
www.heinemann.com

Acknowledgments: Chapter 2, p. 37: "A Wealth of Words: The Key to Increasing Upward Mobility Is Expanding Vocabulary," E. D. Hirsch Jr., *City Journal*. Used with permission of Manhattan Institute for Policy Research, Inc.

Acknowledgments continue on p. viii.

Library of Congress Cataloging-in-Publication Data

Names: Gallagher, Kelly, author.
Title: To read stuff you have to know stuff : helping students build and use prior knowledge / Kelly Gallagher.
Description: Portsmouth, NH : Heinemann, [2025] | Includes bibliographical references and index.
Identifiers: LCCN 2024016072 | ISBN 9780325161464
Subjects: LCSH: Reading comprehension—Study and teaching. | Civics—Study and teaching. | Language arts. | English language—Composition and exercises—Study and teaching.
Classification: LCC LB1050.45 .G37 2025 | DDC 372.47—dc23/eng/20240507
LC record available at https://lccn.loc.gov/2024016072

Printed in the United States of America on acid-free paper
ISBN-13: 978-0-325-16146-4
2 3 4 5 6 7 8 9 10 VP 29 28 27 26

4500930473

Editor: Tom Newkirk
Production: Vicki Kasabian
Permissions: Erika Kane
Cover and text designs: Suzanne Heiser
Typesetting: Kim Arney
Manufacturing: Jaime Spaulding

For those who played

instrumental roles

in building my knowledge

of teaching

Contents

Acknowledgments continued from p. iv:

Chapter 2, p. 37 | The Frayer Model: Used with permission of John Wiley & Sons, from *The Reading Teacher*, vol. 21, issue 7, Dorothy Frayer, Wayne Frederick, Herbert Klausmeier, 1968. Permission conveyed through Copyright Clearance Center, Inc.

Chapter 2, p. 38 | Identifying Words While Reading chart: Used with permission of John Wiley & Sons, from *The ELL Teacher's Toolbox: Hundreds of Practical Ideas to Support Your Students*, Larry Ferlazzo and Katie Hull-Sypnieski, 2018. Permission conveyed through Copyright Clearance Center, Inc.

Chapter 2, p. 58 | *New Yorker* cartoon: © Dan Misdea/The New Yorker Collection/ The Cartoon Bank.

Chapter 2, p. 59 | Mike Lee political cartoon: © Pat Bagley/politicalcartoons.com

Acknowledgments

I could not have written this book without the support of my wife, Kristin, whose contributions to this project and beyond are far too many to list here. Thank you for *everything*.

Thank you to Tom Newkirk, whose influence is present throughout these pages—and throughout my career. Tom not only proposed this project but also edited it. In our frequent discussions, Tom would often say, "You might want to think about . . . ," and then proceed to cite some study from 1948, or a journal article from 1963, or a book from 2024. Thanks, Tom, for being an ideal thought partner and for all you did to elevate this book. In the education world, you are a national treasure. In my world, I am fortunate to have you as a friend.

Much appreciation to the team at Heinemann. Special thanks to Vicki Kasabian, production editor, for overseeing this project; Catrina Swasey, associate managing editor, for attending to endless details; Suzanne Heiser for her beautiful cover and interior design (again!); Elizabeth Marzoli Tripp, for her keen copyediting eye, and Lana Barnes, for her proofreading skills—you both make me look smarter than I am; Erika Kane, for chasing down permissions; Rhonda Medford, for creating the index; and Kim Cahill for her marketing acumen. I also owe a debt of gratitude to the work of Edie Davis Quinn, Cheryl Savage, Tessa Hathaway, Michelle Flynn, and Karen Short—all of whom contributed to the book you are now reading. On the digital side, thank you to Mim Easton for her work in producing the audiobook, and Heather O'Bryan, for overseeing video production. Thanks, as well, to Brett Whitmarsh. I am fortunate to have worked with such a skilled, professional team. Your efforts are deeply appreciated.

Thank you to Robin Turner, Taylor Thorne, Angela Landre, and Kalli Pappas for allowing me into your classrooms. Thanks also to Mike Switzer and Tyler Sherman for your roles in supporting the cross-country book clubs (discussed in Chapter 5) and to Mike Matsuda and Jaron Fried in the Anaheim Union High School District for also lending support for this project.

Thanks to all of you who still believe in the Oxford comma.[1]

As I write in the first chapter, my ability to teach—like yours—is built on what came before. This echoes Alberto Manguel's idea that "everything proceeds in geometric progression based on what is known and what is remembered" (cited in Wolf 2019, 88). This is why, of course, I was a much better teacher at the end of my career than I was in my early years. You have to know stuff to teach stuff, and over time, I learned stuff from my colleagues at Magnolia High School and others in the Anaheim Union High School District. I also learned stuff from the early mentors in my career, most notably John Powers, Jane Davis, Carol Jago, Sheridan Blau, Mary K. Healy, Liz Simon, Jim Burke, Ron Strahl, Nina Wooldridge, Julie Switzer, and Carol Booth Olson. I continued to learn stuff from those I met in later years—Bob Probst, Kylene Beers, Linda Rief, Jeff Wilhelm, Tom Newkirk, Ernest Morrell, Grant Wiggins, Ralph Fletcher, Jeff Anderson, and Donna Santman. And, of course, Penny Kittle. I also learned stuff from those who have written professional books, from teachers who have conducted workshops I have attended, and from the many educators I've met along the road. And, most importantly, I learned stuff—a lot of it—from my two generations of students.

That's a lot of stuff you taught me. Thank you, all.

WORKS CITED

Wolf, Maryanne. 2019. *Reader, Come Home: The Reading Brain in a Digital World.* New York: Harper.

1. Just because.

It is difficult to understand the universe if you study only one planet.
—Miyamoto Musashi
The Book of Five Rings

BUILDING KNOWERS

I discovered the news of Colin Powell's death via this two-sentence news bulletin:

> Colin Powell, the first Black US secretary of state whose leadership in several Republican administrations helped shape American foreign policy in the last years of the 20th century and the early years of the 21st, has died from complications from Covid-19, his family said on Facebook. He was 84. (Cole 2021)

Figure 1–1 shows where my mind went as I read this passage.

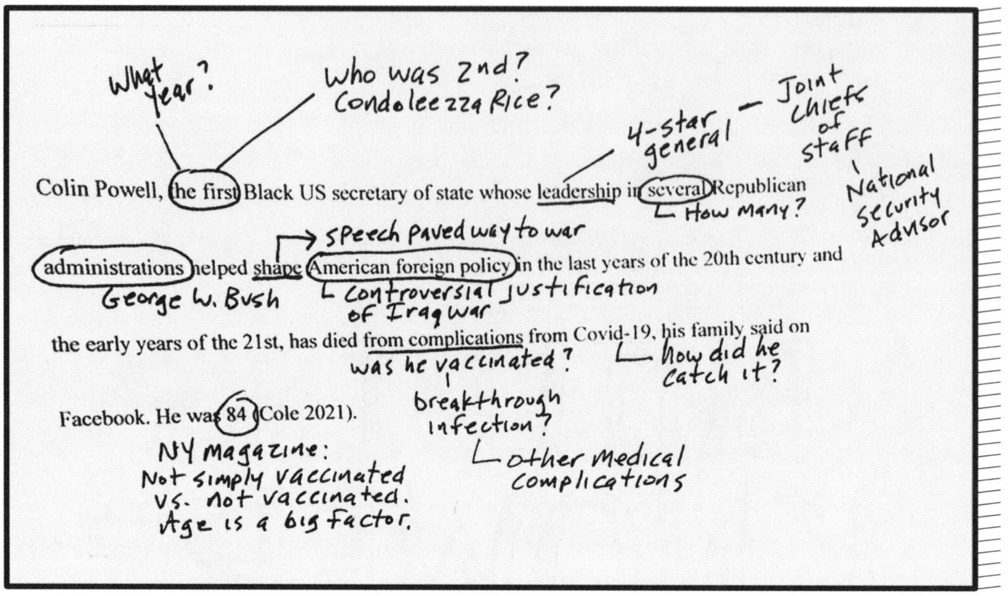
Colin Powell, the first Black US secretary of state whose leadership in several Republican administrations helped shape American foreign policy in the last years of the 20th century and the early years of the 21st, has died from complications from Covid-19, his family said on Facebook. He was 84 (Cole 2021).

Figure 1-1

In reading this short passage, I deepened my comprehension by connecting what I was reading with what I already knew. Specifically, I did the following:

- made a connection to Powell's successor, Condoleezza Rice
- recalled key moments in Powell's military and political career
- remembered his appointment by President George W. Bush (and his subsequent resignation)
- recalled his speech that proffered a controversial justification to pave the way to war (All these years later, I can still visualize exactly where I was sitting while listening to Powell give his infamous speech.)
- considered Powell's vaccination status and wondered whether this may have been a breakthrough infection
- made a connection to an article I recently read about the virus' magnified effect on the elderly
- wondered if Powell had preexisting conditions

When it came to reading about Colin Powell, it was not simply reading the words on the page that led me to deeper reading. *It is what I brought to the page that deepened it.*

This should not come as a surprise to teachers of reading. As Bob Probst (2004) and others have pointed out, it is impossible *not* to apply prior knowledge while reading. (You are most likely using prior knowledge right now as you consider the claim in the previous sentence.) Take the word *Anaheim*, for example. When you see this word, you might think of your first trip to Disneyland. Or it might conjure up an image of a perennially bad Major League Baseball team. Or perhaps the word brings you back to the NCTE conference at the city's convention center. If you live far away, you might be trying to place where the city is located in a mental picture of a map of California. I taught at a high school in Anaheim for thirty-five years—and drove through the city daily—so my understanding of the word is likely much deeper than yours. For any reader, it is impossible to read the word *Anaheim* and not activate *something* in their past. It is this activation that deepens your comprehension.[1]

But what happens when the reader lacks prior knowledge? Let's try another word in isolation. What comes to your mind when you read the word *contig*? My guess? Not much more than *What the heck does* contig *mean?* If you don't know what a contig is, and there is no context to figure it out, it won't matter if you are a proficient reader. It won't matter that you have phonemic awareness or a high degree of fluency. It won't matter if you apply word-attack skills or are highly motivated to figure it out. Your inability to understand the word is rooted in the fact that you have little or no background with the word to draw upon. No strategy from your reader's tool belt is going to help you. Without prior knowledge, making meaning may be impossible. (For the uninitiated, a contig "is a series of overlapping DNA sequences used to make a physical map that reconstructs the original DNA sequence of a chromosome or a region of a chromosome" [Green 2024].)

Now consider a reader who has never heard of Colin Powell. He can read the news bulletin and still learn a few things (e.g., Powell was the first Black secretary of state), but his comprehension will remain at the surface level. He will never understand the queasy feeling I had listening to Powell justify the upcoming invasion of Iraq—a queasiness I felt again (over twenty years later!) when I read of his passing. Reading the text is one thing; being able to read while accessing prior knowledge is another. What we attach to our reading is what gives our comprehension nuance and depth.[2]

---

1. This is something that David Coleman and Sue Pimentel, authors of the Common Core State Standards, got wrong when they suggested that readers should strive to stay within the four corners of the text. As Louise Rosenblatt (1970) famously argued, every reading of a text is a transaction between the text and the reader's unique point of view. To insist readers stay within the four corners of the text "flattens our reading, removes the depth, and erroneously teaches that there is an objective, authorial meaning that you will always be able to discern from the text" (Roberts 2013).

2. When considering the importance of attaching knowledge, we should make a distinction between declarative knowledge and procedural knowledge. What is the difference? *Declarative knowledge* refers to the knowledge of facts or information (e.g., my knowledge of Colin Powell). *Procedural knowledge* is the knowledge of how to do things (e.g., how to make your grandmother's apple pie). Even though we sometimes use both declarative and procedural knowledge in tandem to understand something, the case I make in this book is primarily about the importance of building declarative knowledge in our students. Students need to know things.

Having prior knowledge not only positions you to learn easier and to learn more but also *helps you think about the new information in front of you*. When I read the Colin Powell news, for example, I did not have to spend any cognitive space trying to figure out what the term *secretary of state* meant. I was already aware of his effect on American foreign policy, so thinking about that didn't slow me down. And because I already knew that the COVID virus affected the elderly more severely, I could infer that this may have played a factor in his death, given Powell's advanced age. I didn't simply ingest the information in the passage—my background on the topic opened space for me to think *beyond* the words printed on the page.

THE IMPORTANCE OF OWNING INFORMATION

You may have heard the argument that students don't need to know information because we live in an age where they can just look things up. After all, everything they might need to know is as close as their phones. So, instead of teaching them stuff, what we really should be doing is teaching them how to think.

Well, yes and no.

Certainly, we want to teach students to think critically, but this is not an either-or case. In fact, quite the opposite. Alongside the teaching of critical thinking skills, it is imperative that we also teach kids stuff. Lots of it. Why? *Students who know more are able to learn more, and they are able to learn easier.* Daniel T. Willingham, professor of psychology at the University of Virginia and author of *The Reading Mind: A Cognitive Approach to Understanding How the Mind Reads* (2017) notes that those who possess knowledge find learning less difficult. This is because "factual knowledge enhances cognitive processes like problem-solving and reasoning. The richer the knowledge base, the more smoothly and effectively these cognitive processes—the very ones that teachers target—operate" (Willingham 2006).

There are a number of studies to support this. In one study, David Hambrick (2003) tested college students about their knowledge of basketball during the middle of the season. He tested students again two and one-half months later at the end of the season. Hambrick found students who knew more about basketball prior to the experiment learned more as the season progressed. Having knowledge was a major factor when it came to their learning. Their prior knowledge provided a base and thus enabled them to more easily grow new learning.

These findings are applicable beyond reading about sports. Recht and Leslie (1988) cite studies that came to the same conclusion when students read about diverse topics such as computer programming, electronics, chess, and bridge (as noted by Willingham 2006). Interestingly, the researchers found that both "good" and "poor" readers had similar levels of recall when the text was familiar to them. The "poor" readers, however, were significantly less likely to recall what they read after reading unfamiliar text.

The notion that prior knowledge helps grow new learning is true across the curriculum. In a math class, for example, already knowing how to divide numbers will help you immensely when you are first asked to learn how to compute percentages. In a social studies class, you cannot glean a deep understanding of the Russian invasion of Ukraine or the Israel-Hamas war unless you possess knowledge of the history of those regions. In an earth science class, a deeper understanding of earthquakes comes to those who already possess an understanding of the architecture of the earth. And so on.

Additionally, prior knowledge not only plays a critical role when it comes to reading but also plays an even more crucial role when it comes to writing. As I said, you may know nothing about Colin Powell before reading about him, but you will still be able to understand some of what you are reading. But if you sit down to write about Colin Powell—and you know nothing about him—you are dead in the water. It is not a coincidence that almost all my best high school writers were students who had broad reading backgrounds. You have to know stuff to read stuff, but you *really* have to know stuff to write stuff.

☆—☆—☆

A few years ago I taught a digital composition unit to my ninth-grade students. I asked them to make two-minute films. For many of these freshmen, this was the first time they had ever attempted to make a movie, so there was a steep learning curve. Understandably, there was a lot of trial and error, and, as expected, a lot of mistakes were made. As novices, they learned plenty, but many of their finished products were rough and elementary.

One year later, I repeated this unit with the same students (they had looped with me, meaning they were my students again in tenth grade). When the tenth-grade unit was complete, I was stunned at the advancement many of them had made from the previous year. When I say their films were markedly better, I don't mean they got better at making simplistic films. I mean their *level of attempt* at filmmaking grew more sophisticated. Not only did they get better at the skills they had struggled with the previous year, but they attempted new things. Ernesto, who had previously only printed captions on the screen, was now infusing voice-overs. Jasmin, who told a straightforward story as a ninth grader, was now weaving in graphics in key spots. Kelsey went from using one song in her film to blending songs from different artists to match different segments.

Why were these students so much better in their second lap of filmmaking? For one thing, they didn't come to the task cold. They had internalized much of what they had learned from the previous year's trial and error, thus enabling them to begin the new unit at a more elevated starting place. Filmmaking is complex; one does not learn to make a polished film in one attempt. The students learned a lot in lap one, and then they added to what they had learned in lap two. Beginning the unit in year two with some knowledge launched them to new levels of learning.

This concept of learning in laps is something that Penny Kittle and I discuss in our book *180 Days* (Gallagher and Kittle 2018). When teaching narrative writing, for example, we did not try to teach all skills in one essay. We started small and worked up from there. In the first lap, we taught students how to infuse sensory details into their writing. Once they had that skill down, we had them write a second piece that included sensory detail but added the use of dialogue. Once they learned how to add dialogue, we had them write a third piece that included sensory detail, dialogue, and the use of strong voice. In a fourth lap, we taught them how to flash forward or flash back in their narratives. Rather than trying to teach all things in one paper, we took a building-block approach—we taught one skill and once students gained ownership of that one skill, we built on top of their newly acquired knowledge. We added knowledge in a sequenced approach. Knowing how to do A made it easier to learn B. And so on.

PRIOR KNOWLEDGE AND TEACHING

To further underscore the importance that prior knowledge plays in learning, let's consider how a good teacher became a good teacher.

First, of course, there was a lot of trial and error. When I was a young teacher and I didn't get an immediate answer to a question I posed in class, I quickly defaulted to panic mode. It took me a few years to learn the value of wait time—to live with the presence of silence. I came to realize that students would often remain mute *on purpose*, hoping the silence would make me so uncomfortable that I'd break down and answer my own question.

Smart, those kids.

But this is just one of a million things that I had to learn the hard way. Writing this has triggered another memory: I was a first-year teacher, and I had learned in my credential program that it was important for students to hear models of good oral language. I was teaching a sophomore honors class, and I decided to read a key chapter of *To Kill a Mockingbird* to the class.[3] I was nervous, but I had practiced the night before, and the reading went off without a hitch. Or so I thought. The next day I stepped into the hallway during the passing period, and when I entered the room at the beginning of class, someone had taped a paper cutout of me to my podium with the words "Mr. Mono" written across my chest.

Subtle, those kids.

As painful as that experience was, it taught me something valuable that I carried throughout the rest of my career—that reading in front of kids needs to be a *performance*. This was a call to up my game. The next year I read Atticus' closing argument aloud and got so into it I was on the verge of tears, so I may have overcompensated. But, perhaps not—as some of my students were choked up as well.

These are only two examples of what I needed to learn early in my teaching career. There were so many others. Years later, when I worked with student teachers, I was frequently reminded just how much there is to learn. I was struck by how much the new teachers did not know. This is not a criticism, as many of them were excellent; rather, it was a reminder of just how many things a person learns on the way to becoming an experienced teacher. We often forget how much we have learned in our craft.[4]

Beyond trial and error, a second important element to becoming a good teacher is the development of one's teaching DNA. By "teaching DNA," I mean the influences on your craft that come from outside the walls of your classroom and how those influences have been remixed and mashed up to compose your makeup as a teacher. As Austin Kleon, author of *Steal Like an Artist*, says in a widely viewed TED talk, "Nothing is completely original. All creative work builds on what came before. Every new idea is a remix or mash-up of one or two previous ideas" (2012).

My ability to teach—like yours—is built on what came before. It is built from the veteran teachers who gave me advice based on their experiences. It is built from all the professional books I have read. It is built from the teaching conferences I attended. Each time I discussed teaching with a mentor, or read a book about how to teach writing, or attended the yearly NCTE conference, my skill set grew and evolved. I didn't

---

3. All these years later, I have come to see the teaching of *To Kill a Mockingbird* as problematic. But this anecdote occurred many years ago, and I had not evolved to my current thinking.

4. Student teachers often struggle because they don't know what they don't know.

just magically emerge as a skilled teacher. My craft was constructed from a long lineage of teaching ideas—a teaching family tree, if you will. I acquired knowledge from others, gained ownership of this knowledge, and then built upon it.[5] For the best teachers I know, this cycle never ends.[6]

BUILDING A WEB OF KNOWLEDGE

When I read that Colin Powell had died, George Orwell's *Animal Farm* immediately came to mind. Recalling Powell's infamous speech justifying the US invasion of Iraq reminded me of the speeches given by the pigs on the farm to garner support from the other animals. Both used propaganda to sway the masses. And when I started thinking of this manipulation of the masses, I automatically made connections to other dystopian books, like *1984*, *Fahrenheit 451*, *The Hunger Games*, *The Handmaid's Tale*, *The Children of Men*, and *In Order to Live: A North Korean Girl's Journey to Freedom*. And thinking of those books prompted me to recall thematically similar films, like *Blade Runner*, *The Matrix*, *Soylent Green*, *The Truman Show*, and *Minority Report*.[7] And thinking of those films led me to think about the propaganda that Vladimir Putin uses with the Russian citizenry to justify his invasion of Ukraine. And thinking about Putin's tactics reminded me of propaganda other nations have made to justify starting wars. And on and on. One thought connects with another, which connects to another.

Teachers of reading will recognize that what I am doing here is making text-to-world connections—a skill we want all of our young readers to develop. I connected the reading of the Colin Powell article to numerous other cultural artifacts and events. I was able to do this because I have a reservoir of prior knowledge that helps me construct this web of connections. But you can't make a text-to-text connection if you haven't read other texts. And you can't make a text-to-world connection if you have been stuck in an entertainment silo and haven't been "reading" the world. Building

5. On the first page of *4 Essential Studies*, Penny Kittle and I (2022) created a graphic depicting the educators who influenced us throughout the years. There are over 125 educators named.

6. David Dockterman, a teacher at Harvard University and proficient author, once told me his favorite question to ask teachers of all levels of experience is "What is the next best thing to learn?"

7. *The Minority Report*, directed by Steven Spielberg, is underrated. And even though Spielberg is one of the most renowned directors of all time, he has made other films that remain underappreciated (e.g., *Munich* and *The Sugarland Express*). The fact that *Saving Private Ryan* lost the Oscar for best picture to *Shakespeare in Love* is an injustice. Don't DM me.

a rich, connective web is not possible if you don't have a knowledge base to anchor these connections.

So asking a student without schemata to make a text-to-text connection is problematic. Here are four other reading strategies that may be troublesome without the possession of prior knowledge.

Visualizing

Teachers teach students to create mental pictures or movies in their minds as they read. Try visualizing this passage from John Knowles' *A Separate Peace*, which describes a New England boarding school in the 1940s:

> **Devon is sometimes considered the most beautiful school in New England, and even on this dismal afternoon its power was asserted. It is the beauty of small areas of order—a large yard, a group of trees, three similar dormitories, a circle of old houses—living together in contentious harmony. You felt that an argument might begin again at any time; in fact it had: out of the Dean's Residence, a pure and authentic Colonial house, there now sprouted an ell with a big, bare picture window. (1959, 13)**

Many of my students had never been out of Southern California, so asking them to visualize this passage would have been highly problematic. A "circle of old houses" in Anaheim looks very different from a circle of old houses built over a hundred years ago in New England. My students lived in cookie-cutter tract homes and apartments. Would they know what an "authentic Colonial house" looked like? And given the fact that many of them had never visited a school where students lived on campus, it is likely they would have had trouble visualizing a prep school dormitory.

It's hard, if not impossible, to visualize without prior knowledge of the subject.

Questioning

According to the Texas Education Agency, "the ability of readers to ask themselves relevant questions as they read is especially valuable in helping them to integrate information, identify main ideas, and summarize information. Asking the right questions allows good readers to focus on the most important information in a text" (2002).

But what are the right questions?

I once heard my friend Sheridan Blau[8] suggest that there are three essential questions we want to teach all readers to answer:

> What does it say?
>
> What does it mean?
>
> Why does it matter? [9]

With these questions in mind, read the following passage:

> **In physics, string theory is a theoretical framework in which the point-like particles of particle physics are replaced by one-dimensional objects called strings. String theory describes how these strings propagate through space and interact with each other. On distance scales larger than the string scale, a string looks just like an ordinary particle, with its mass, charge, and other properties determined by the vibrational state of the string. In string theory, one of the many vibrational states of the string corresponds to the graviton, a quantum mechanical particle that carries the gravitational force. Thus, string theory is a theory of quantum gravity. (Wikimedia Foundation 2024)[10]**

I have read this passage several times and I still struggle to understand it. I am definitely wrestling with it on a "What does it say?" level. Because of my lack of prior knowledge, my questions are very surface level: What does "point-like particles" mean? What is a "vibrational state of the string"? You should know that the bold words in this passage indicate hyperlinks that provide the reader with helpful prior knowledge—thirteen links to help you understand one paragraph! Confession: I read every one of those links in trying to understand this passage.

What a slog.

Now let's consider Blau's other questions: What does it mean? Why does it matter? These questions require inference from the reader, which is next to impossible if the reader is in "What does it say?" survival mode. How can I say what it really means or why it really matters if I don't have more than an elemental understanding of what it says? I can't question how string theory might have contributed to the advancement

---

8. Blau is a former president of NCTE and has just retired after a sixty-four-year teaching career. (That's not a typo—sixty-four years!) If you haven't read him, I recommend starting with his book *The Literature Workshop*.

9. Given the events of recent years, I would add two more questions: Who said it? Do we trust this source?

10. Passages like this remind me why I was an English major.

in mathematical physics without possessing background knowledge about string theory (or about mathematical physics). Another confession: I couldn't even write the previous sentence without looking up this connection online.

It's hard, if not impossible, to ask rich questions without prior knowledge of the subject. And this applies outside of the text as well. It helps to know what to ask before walking into a car dealership to buy a new car. Or before challenging your landlord, your principal, or your congresswoman. Or when deciding on how best to get your hands on Taylor Swift tickets.[11]

Predicting

Last night I went to a Los Angeles Angels of Anaheim baseball game.[12] The Angels have a promising young player, Jo Adell, who is struggling to make his mark in the Major leagues. In the fifth inning, Adell had two strikes on him. I turned to my wife, Kristin, and said, "He will strike out on a low slider outside of the strike zone." On the next pitch, sure enough, he struck out on a low slider outside of the strike zone. This prediction was not wild luck, and to the best of my knowledge, I am not a direct descendent of Nostradamus. This prediction was tied to the fact that I have watched Adell strike out numerous times in the past month, always on low sliders off the plate. He simply cannot lay off them. And if I know this, the other team certainly knows this. My prediction was not brilliant; it was grounded in the pain of watching a lot of Angels games.

This grounding in background knowledge is often missing when I ask students to make predictions while they are reading a novel. You've done this, right? You get your students to a key point in the book and you ask them to predict what happens next. Here's the good news: they can readily make predictions. The bad news is that their predictions are often devoid of any underlying reason or insight. I once asked a student why he predicted that the main character would die. He stared at me for a few seconds and finally said, "That would be a rad ending."

Well, yes. But what *led you* to that conclusion?

Much like I would not have been able to predict that Jo Adell would strike out unless I had watched a lot of his at bats over time, students who have not read a lot of books are less likely to catch foreshadowing along the way. Experienced readers become skilled at recognizing key moments in the text. For example, Beers and Probst (2013) teach readers to look for "memory moments"—recollections by a character that

---

11. Good luck.

12. *The Los Angeles Angels of Anaheim* is the lamest rebranding since Coca-Cola foisted New Coke upon us.

interrupt the forward progress of the story (this is one of six signposts they identify for readers). These interruptions are often clues to big ideas that will emerge later. Similarly, I have heard Jeff Wilhelm say that readers should keep an eye out for "fractures" in the text, saying that when the flow of the chapter is interrupted, this usually means that the author wants you to stop and pay closer attention. There are hints lurking in these fractures.

It's hard, if not impossible, to make meaningful predictions without tons of reading experience. The more you read, the more knowledge you garner about how plots are constructed and what clues are embedded in the text. I have read countless crime novels, for example, and I have become skilled at predicting what comes next. There's a certain feel to this genre. My ability to accurately predict has developed because I have read hundreds of mysteries.[13]

Inferring

In William Golding's *Lord of the Flies* (1954), Simon always puts others first, and he has a spiritual connection to nature (as evidenced by the "candle buds"). He is meditative, has bright eyes (indicating vision and truth), and shares a prophecy with Ralph, one of the boys on the island. He is the only inherently good character in the novel, and he alone confronts evil (the Lord of the Flies). When he tries to bring his message of hope to the boys, he is misunderstood and ultimately sacrificed. His body washes into the sea, and phosphorescent creatures form a halo effect around his head. The inference is clear—Simon is a Christ-like figure—but making this inference is contingent on knowing the story of Jesus. Again, you have to know stuff to deeply read stuff.

When people (or characters) wrongly infer, it usually means they lack enough context. When Romeo finds Juliet in a deep, drug-induced sleep, he wrongly infers that the pressures put upon her by her family proved to be too much. He believes she has taken her life, so, tragically, he follows suit. Romeo has no knowledge of the friar's plan, and his lack of understanding of the big picture leads to tragedy. (Which raises an interesting question for readers of the play: Was Romeo's inference reasonable?)

Beyond literature, the ability to infer insightfully in the real world is also tied to having prior knowledge. When my wife, Kristin, was eight days overdue in her first pregnancy, I got *the call* from her. She was crying hysterically, telling me she had gone into labor and that I needed to get home *now*! Panicked, I sprinted to my car, jumped

---

13. My ability to make accurate predictions holds true for crime series on television, as well. So much so that I usually take delight when I am wrong. Usually, but not always. A note to the makers of *Ozark*: You killed the wrong character in the final episode! How dare you?!

on the freeway, broke every driving law known to humankind, and fifteen minutes later skidded into our driveway. I had inferred from the desperation in her voice that I might discover her delivering this baby on the kitchen floor. She had sounded that bad on the phone. As I ran to the front door, I was already wondering what I would use to cut the umbilical cord.

When I rushed into the house, Kristin was nowhere to be found. I called out her name. No response. My heart was jackhammering! And then, ever so faintly, I could hear the water running in the back bathroom. I ran to the rear of the house, where I found my wife singing merrily in the shower. Singing! Merrily! "Oh, hi," she said cheerfully. "If I'm going to have this baby today, I thought I'd take a shower and clean up before heading to the hospital!"[14]

What the hell just happened?

You see, I had inferred the birth was imminent because of the level of panic in her voice on that phone call. My inference was wrong, however, because I was unaware that mood swings induced by pregnancy *can intensify significantly* when a woman goes into labor.[15] I lacked this critical tidbit of prior knowledge, which led me to dangerously impersonate a Formula One driver as I raced down the 5 freeway in a frenzied panic. It turned out there was no hurry: my daughter, Caitlin, was born *thirteen* hours later.

Inferring is much easier when you know things.

KNOWLEDGE COLLECTION BEGINS IN INFANCY

As a longtime high school teacher, I contend that a major problem with building thoughtful readers in secondary classrooms is that many students lack the prior knowledge needed to reach comprehension. Yes, they can read. They can pronounce the words. They have developed enough fluency or automaticity to free up cognitive space to think about their reading. But they are often missing the background knowledge necessary to comprehend. For example, I have shown students a meme that depicts Vincent van Gogh's self-portrait. Dangling from his left ear is a COVID-19 mask. The caption reads, "Oh crap." If students don't know that Van

14. Thus confirming Robert Louis Stevenson's central theme of duality in *Dr. Jekyll and Mr. Hyde*.

15. This lesson was clearly reinforced again in the labor room, but enough said. The point has been made.

Gogh cut off his other ear in a fit of madness, they will never understand the meme no matter how effortlessly they read it.

But a lack of prior knowledge is a problem not just for secondary readers. This is an issue that affects readers long before middle and high school. In fact, long before kindergarten. Numerous studies have found that early (ages one through five) academic skills related to literacy and math are the most significant predictors of future academic achievement (Hanover Research 2016). In other words, *there is often a strong correlation between a child's level of literacy when she enters kindergarten and her level of literacy when she exits the twelfth grade.* To understand how this might be, allow me to take a small detour by referring to Malcom Gladwell's *Outliers* (2008), where the author uncovered a strange pattern when looking at the birthdays of professional Canadian hockey players. Gladwell noted a disproportionate number of NHL players were born in the first three months of the calendar year.

Why might this be?

Gladwell discovered that coaches start identifying the best young players as early as eight or nine, and that the eligibility cutoff for age-class hockey programs was the end of the calendar year. This means that the best players at age eight are usually those born at the beginning of the year. An eight-year-old born in January can be almost a year older than an eight-year-old born in December. These ten or eleven extra months of physical maturity gave these young players an edge. They were thus more likely to be recruited and placed into elite programs—yes, even at this young age—where they'd play a lot more games and receive better coaching. Because these advantages accelerated quickly, these players were more likely to turn professional years later.

Gladwell's anecdote highlights the advantage that some youngsters have in *physical* maturity. But Gladwell's hockey story reminds me of numerous conversations I have had with kindergarten teachers who told me that some students start kindergarten knowing a lot more than their peers. Like the age differences in the hockey example, there are "young" five-year-olds and there are "old" five-year-olds when it comes to their levels of literacy. Reading abilities of incoming kindergartners cover about a five-year span, from that of a typical three-year-old to that of a typical eight-year-old (Loveless 2021). A national study conducted by the US Department of Education found that older five-year-olds who enter kindergarten with advanced skills are closer to being able to read, are closer to being able to do arithmetic, and know more about nature, science, and human society (2001). They also have more advanced motor skills, are more socially adept, and exhibit a more positive approach to learning. These students have gained more ownership of words and knowledge, which in turn gives them more confidence—an advantage that later helps propel them into gifted tracks.

Although this book is about the importance prior knowledge plays in developing readers, it helps to know that knowledge acquisition begins long before kids actually learn to read. According to the National Association for the Education of Young Children,

> **from infancy through age 8, proactively building children's conceptual and factual knowledge, including academic vocabulary, is essential because knowledge is the primary driver of comprehension. The more children (and adults) know, the better their listening comprehension and, later, reading comprehension. *By building knowledge of the world in early childhood, educators are laying the foundation that is critical for all future learning.* (NAEYC 2019, 14; italics mine)**

The accumulation of factual knowledge—the knowledge critical to building readers—begins in infancy.[16]

☆–☆–☆

It is astonishing—and a bit daunting—to realize that a child's readiness (or lack of readiness) when *entering* kindergarten plays a strong role in determining her twelfth-grade outcome. This raises anxiety in teachers, as a child's background is something we cannot control. We stand at our classroom doors on the first day of school and welcome students who possess a wide range of experiences and abilities. The last twelfth-grade class I taught, for example, had readers reading at far below grade level mixed with students reading at a college level. These gaps make teaching extraordinarily challenging.

This wide range of abilities found in our students reminds me of a horrific story an early-elementary teacher told me. Her school planned a field trip to the zoo for all the second graders, but as the day approached, budgets were slashed in half, and they had to revise their plans. So instead of canceling the trip, they made the mind-boggling decision to take half the students on the field trip. That's right, half—which meant, of course, that the other half would not be going. And here is where it gets worse: The school's leader decided to take the "top" half of their students, as a reward based on some sort of measurement of academic achievement. The "bottom" half was left behind.

16. Another reason to support programs like Head Start, which have been proven to have significant benefits to children (Bitler, Hoynes, and Domina 2014).

This is wrong on so many levels—far too many to get into here. But if I had been a teacher forced into that situation, I would have argued strenuously that the administration had gotten the decision backward. They should have taken the lowest-achieving students, the kids who were "behind" and thus more likely to have gaps in their prior knowledge. (As you may have surmised, many of the students left behind had never been to a zoo.) These kids needed as many knowledge-building opportunities as possible.

The zoo story has one more twist. A year later, the teacher moved across town to teach at a school in a much more affluent neighborhood. Her new students had access to a lot more books at home. This school, too, decided to take its second graders to the zoo, and they had the budget to take everyone. Almost every one of these students had already been to the zoo, and during the visit, the teacher was astonished at just how much more insightful her students' comments and questions were compared with those of her students from the previous school. Teaching in these two schools, she said, was like teaching in separate universes.

We all teach students who come from separate universes. And while we cannot control what happens to them before they come to us, we can be intentional about helping them build background knowledge that is foundational to becoming thoughtful readers.

☆–☆–☆

When I look at the catalogs of the publishers of educational books, they are mostly filled with strategy-heavy books. Why? These books sell well. Teachers (myself included) love to learn new strategies. But the pendulum has swung too far in this direction. Strategies are great—for both teachers and students—but in many cases (e.g., making a text-to-text connection, visualizing, questioning, inferring) they may be useless to the reader (or writer) who doesn't possess background knowledge. A curriculum that focuses on teaching strategies without an equal emphasis on building knowledge is out of balance. You can teach strategies, but they won't help or work unless we also build *knowers*.

That is what this book is about. Building knowers.

In Chapter 2, we will examine the role prior knowledge plays at the word level, and in doing so, we will look at how to help students overcome word poverty.

In Chapter 3, we will explore what teachers can do to help students become better readers (and writers) of sentences and passages.

In Chapter 4, we will consider how to help students build a knowledge base that will help them read critically at the article level.

In Chapter 5, we will appraise the importance that prior knowledge plays when reading books, and in doing so, we will look at ways to help students develop the ability to tackle longer works.

We will conclude in Chapter 6 by examining the implications for planning and instruction. Saying we should build knowledge in students is one thing. Doing so raises a thorny issue: What knowledge—and whose knowledge—should we teach?

But before we move to Chapter 2, let's remember three key points made in this chapter:

1. Students who know more are able to read easier.
2. Students who know more are able to read more.
3. Students who know more are able to think about their reading at a deeper level because they can more readily make connections.

Clearly, when it comes to learning, *owning knowledge is much better than having to look things up*. As Willingham notes, "looking up information is a poor substitute for knowing that information when you are reading: first, it's often difficult to find the right bit of information the author intended, and second, it turns reading into problem solving and so incurs a significant cognitive cost" (2017, 167). The more students know, the more they can read. The more they can read, the more they will read. The more they will read, the more they will know. The more they will know, the more they can read. An endless positive loop that builds reading identity and agency is established. The rich get richer.

This is why this is not simply a strategy book. Building adolescent readers starts with building knowers.

WORKS CITED

Beers, Kylene, and Robert E. Probst. 2013. *Notice and Note: Strategies for Close Reading*. Portsmouth, NH: Heinemann.

Bitler, Marianne P., Hilary W. Hoynes, and Thurston Domina. 2014. "Experimental Evidence on Distributional Effects of Head Start." Working paper 20434. National Bureau of Economic Research, Issue Date: August.

Cole, Devan. 2021. "Colin Powell, First Black US Secretary of State, Dies of Covid-19 Complications amid Cancer Battle." CNN. Updated October 19. https://www.cnn.com/2021/10/18/politics/colin-powell-dies/index.html.

Gallagher, Kelly, and Penny Kittle. 2018. *180 Days: Two Teachers and the Quest to Engage and Empower Adolescents*. Portsmouth, NH: Heinemann.

Gladwell, Malcolm. 2019. *Outliers: The Story of Success*. New York: Little, Brown.

Golding, William. 1954. *Lord of the Flies*. London, UK: Faber and Faber.

Green, Eric. 2024. "Contig." National Human Genome Research Institute. Updated March 7. https://www.genome.gov/genetics-glossary/Contig.

Hambrick, David Z. 2003. "Why Are Some People More Knowledgeable Than Others? A Longitudinal Study of Knowledge Acquisition." *Memory and Cognition* 31: 902–17. https://link.springer.com/article/10.3758/BF03196444.

Hanover Research. 2016. *Early Skills and Predictors of Academic Success*. Arlington, VA: Hanover Research. https://portal.ct.gov/-/media/SDE/ESSA-Evidence-Guides/Early_Skills_and_Predictors_of_Academic_Success.

Kittle, Penny, and Kelly Gallagher. 2022. *4 Essential Studies: Beliefs and Practices to Reclaim Student Agency*. Portsmouth, NH: Heinemann.

Kleon, Austin. 2012. "Steal Like an Artist: Austin Kleon at TEDxKC." TEDx Talks, April 24. YouTube video, 11:14. https://www.youtube.com/watch?v=oww7oB9rjgw.

Knowles, John. 1959. *A Separate Peace*. New York: Scribner.

Loveless, Tom. 2021. "Why Common Core Failed." Brookings. March 18. https://www.brookings.edu/articles/why-common-core-failed/.

National Center for Education Statistics. 2001. "Entering Kindergarten: Findings from the Condition of Education 2000."

Probst, Robert E. 2004. *Response and Analysis: Teaching Literature in Secondary School*. Portsmouth, NH: Heinemann.

Recht, Donna R., and Lauren Leslie. 1988. "Effect of Prior Knowledge on Good and Poor Readers' Memory of Text." *Journal of Educational Psychology* 80 (1): 16–20.

Roberts, Kate. 2013. "The Five Corners of the Text: Close Reading and Personal Experience." *Kate & Maggie* (blog), September 5. https://www.kateandmaggie.com/the-content-shop-free-blog/2013/09/05/the-five-corners-of-the-text-close-reading-and-personal-experience.

Rosenblatt, Louise M. 1970. *Literature as Exploration*. New York: Random House. First published 1938.

Texas Education Agency. 2002. "Key Comprehension Strategies to Teach." Reading Rockets. https://www.readingrockets.org/topics/comprehension/articles/key-comprehension-strategies-teach.

Wikimedia Foundation. 2024. "String Theory." Wikipedia. Last edited February 12. https://en.wikipedia.org/wiki/String_theory.

Willingham, Daniel T. 2006. "How Knowledge Helps." *American Educator* (Spring): 30–34, 36–37. https://www.aft.org/ae/spring2006/willingham.

———. 2017. *The Reading Mind: A Cognitive Approach to Understanding How the Mind Reads*. San Francisco: Jossey-Bass.

2

Owning words makes it easier to connect with new learning.

WORDS, WORDS, WORDS

Years ago, I heard the author Judith Ortiz Cofer say that words are weapons and tools. I thought about this statement every time I taught George Orwell's *1984* (1949)—a dystopian novel written in the shadow of the totalitarian regimes that rose to power in World War II. In the novel, the Ministry of Truth, a government agency that constantly lies, actively works to reduce the number of words in the English language. Every new edition of the Newspeak dictionary contains fewer words. Instead of words like *good*, *excellent*, and *superlative*, the dictionary contains words like *good*, *plusgood*, and *doubleplusgood*. The goal is the destruction of words, because when people suffer from word poverty, they suffer from idea poverty. Limiting words limits their thinking.[1] And when their thinking is limited, they are less equipped to criticize their government.

Unfortunately, there is ample evidence that many of our students suffer from word poverty, particularly those who come from economically disadvantaged households. Brenda J. Overturf, Leslie H. Montgomery, and Margot Holmes Smith, in *Word Nerds*, note:

> **Hart and Risley (1995) conducted a major study of the number of words children learn by age three and found huge**

1. This is evident when we look at how many times in history that repressive regimes have banned books and restricted information—and as I write this, book banning is rampant in the United States. More on this later.

> differences between those from affluent families and those from low-income families. The results were so startling that the report is often called the Meaningful Difference study because Hart and Risley wrote about a "30-million word gap" between children from professional families and children from economically-disadvantaged households. (2013, 8)[2]

This gap correlates with later school achievement. Kids with broader vocabularies get ahead more quickly and achieve more (Stanovich 1984). Hirsch (2013) also found that "there's a positive correlation between a student's vocabulary size in grade 12, the likelihood that she will graduate from college, and her future level of income."

But it would be a mistake to think that word poverty is a problem only for kids from economically disadvantaged households. Word poverty affects a wide swath of Americans. Surprisingly, one study found that the largest decrease in vocabulary is actually found in adults with bachelor's or graduate degrees (see Heingartner 2020). (Not surprisingly, a similar decrease was also found among people who did not attend college.) Why this drop across different demographics? The researchers suggest there may be a number of causes: a decline in reading, the overuse of emojis for written communication, "or, more generally, perhaps American culture itself has become 'less intellectual, either because of or in response to a lowering of verbal ability among those who read books'" (Heingartner 2020). These findings are supported by Scholastic's "Kids and Family Reading Report," which since 2010 has explored the reading habits of children ages six through seventeen. The 2019 study found an "overall decline of children reading nearly every day (frequent readers), and a rise in those reading less than 1 day a week (infrequent readers)."

And this study was conducted before the pandemic. Things seem worse now. I have spoken to a number of teachers who believe their students did very little reading while away from school for up to two years, and this habit of not reading has remained prevalent in students sitting in their classrooms today. Word poverty is growing.

2. This study is not without critics. Some argue that "the study favors White, upper- and middle-class speech norms and focuses exclusively on conversations between parent and child that do not account for cultural differences in how families interact and communicate" (Williams 2020).

OVERCOMING WORD POVERTY

Not knowing a word in a sentence can limit your understanding far beyond that single word. Take this sentence from Louis Rosenblatt's seminal work, *Literature as Exploration*:[3]

> **Certainly, lively, untrammeled conversation bespeaks an admirable educational setting. (1970, 75)**

If you don't know the meaning of *untrammeled*, you might still be able to decipher the general gist of the sentence, as you might recognize it as an adjective describing conversation. But if you don't know the meaning of *bespeaks*, your ability to understand the rest of the sentence is greatly diminished.

One sign that students suffer from word poverty is their misuse of the thesaurus. You know what this looks like. The sentence "She had strong feelings" gets revised to "She had impregnable feelings." The newly chosen word doesn't quite fit correctly, and it doesn't sound anything like the student's authentic voice. This is why I always had my students follow the rule I learned from my colleague Nina Woolridge: When using a thesaurus, select only your friends; stay away from strangers. This is harder to do, of course, when students have very few word friends.[4]

When thinking about how to build our students' vocabularies, it helps to consider the following big ideas.

We Learn Words Incrementally

Sometimes when a student encounters an unfamiliar word, the context is very strong and they are able to make a reasonable guess as to its meaning. Take the following example:

> **His fatuous comments made it clear he didn't know what he was talking about.**

---

3. It has been my experience that many teachers new to the profession are unfamiliar with this groundbreaking book. If you haven't read it, put it at the top of your list of professional books to read.

4. This is also why it is easier to detect plagiarism in writers who suffer from word poverty—the shift in voice is painfully obvious. Writing produced by ChatGPT often doesn't match student voice—a sure sign the piece was not written by the adolescent. I always marveled at students who cut and pasted the work of others without matching the font to what they had already written. C'mon, really?

The context is strong enough in this sentence that a reader would most likely infer that *fatuous* means foolish, uneducated, or inane. But what if the reader's first encounter with *fatuous* were found instead in this sentence:

They were tired of his fatuous comments.

Here, the context is much more ambiguous. From this sentence, the reader might logically but wrongfully infer that *fatuous* means inflammatory or long-winded. Or the reader might sort of get its meaning but need to see the word in other contexts before fully grasping it.

Often, we learn words incrementally. Dale (1965, 898) suggests stages on a continuum, as shown in Figure 2–1. Next to these stages I share my own examples.

We Learn Words Through Multiple Exposures

When I taught students a new word—*diction*, for example—I was intentional about providing as much context around the word as possible. After introducing the word and its definition, I said something like the following: "As we read this passage from Julie Otsuka's *The Swimmers*, I'd like you to pay close attention to her diction. Her word choices are interesting. In this passage, she describes various people in her

Stages of How We Learn Words	Examples from My Life
"I never saw it before."	***Engrail***: I do not recall seeing this word.
"I've heard of it, but I don't know what it means."	***Lugubrious***: I have a sense that it has a negative connotation, but I can't quite define it.
"I recognize it in context—it has something to do with . . ."	***Cytology***: I know by its suffix that it is the study of something, but I'm not sure what.
"I know it."	***Ubiquitous***: I am comfortable using this word in various contexts.

Figure 2–1

neighborhood who swim in the community underground pool. What do you notice about her word choice—her diction—in this passage?"

> **Above ground many of us are ungainly and awkward, slowing down with the years. The extra poundage has arrived, the letting go has begun, the crow's-feet are fanning out silently, but inexorably, like cracks on a windshield, from the corner of our eyes. But down below, at the pool, we are restored to our old youthful selves. Gray hairs vanish beneath dark blue swim caps. Brows unfurrow. Limps disappear. Kettle-bellied men with knee woes on land bob daintily up and down in their bright orange flotation belts as they aqua-jog in place. (2022, 10)**

After reading the passage, I said: "As we look at her diction, I'd like you to zoom in on one decision she made about word choice that you find interesting. I'll go first: I am interested in her use of the word *kettle-bellied*. What an interesting choice of diction! Why not just say *large*, *rotund*, or *heavy*? Why do you think she made this decision? Why this specific choice?"

After discussing my choice, I asked students to zoom in on "hot spots" of their own. Where else in the passage did they find interesting word choices? Why did they think Otsuka made these choices? I asked them to share their thinking, and as they did so I was sure to work the word *diction* into the conversation numerous times (e.g., "I like the diction you noticed, Isabelle."). By the end of the class period, my students heard the word *diction* used in context several times.[5]

It is the repetition that is important. McKeown et al. (1985) found that students who were exposed to a word twelve times were much more likely to learn it than students who had only four encounters. Shanahan (2016) notes that other studies "suggest that the number of repetitions needed to learn a word is about 10–15 times, with lots of variation—among kids and words. For example, poor readers may require 12–25 reps to 'learn' a word, while better readers may get away with only 8–12."[6]

Readers learn words incrementally. Multiple exposures are necessary to move readers from partial to full ownership. Hirsch (2013) notes,

> **The sense of a word that a listener or reader gains from multiple exposures to it isn't a fixed and definite meaning but rather a system**

---

5. Lesson idea: Have students read for ten minutes, and then have them analyze the author's choice of one specific word.

6. Shanahan cites a study by Lemoine, Levy, and Hutchison (1993) to arrive at these numbers. See works cited.

> of meaning *possibilities* that get narrowed down through context on each occasion. . . . Knowledge of a word is a memory residue of several meaningful encounters with the word in diverse contexts. We retain bits of those past contexts in memory as part of the word's meaning-potential. Almost all the word meanings that we know are acquired indirectly by intuitively guessing new meanings as we get the overall gist of what we're hearing or reading.

We Learn Words in Waves

Through extensive analysis of word usage, researchers know we learn new words in waves. In a 2022 conversation with vocabulary expert Elfrieda Hiebert, I learned that some words come to us as early readers and then are left behind. *Balloon*, for example, appears often in early-grade texts but is rarely seen in texts after grade five. Words like *suffice* and *articulate*, on the other hand, arrive in a later wave—they do not emerge until high school–level text. And then there are words that arrive early but stay with us—the word *relieved*, for example, emerges in third-grade texts and remains constant in grade-level texts through the twelfth grade.

The amount of words students learn in the early waves deeply influences how many words they may learn in the later waves. Hiebert suggests that readers who read at a 92 percent accuracy level or higher are much more likely to make meaning when confronted with unfamiliar words. Students reading below this threshold struggle as they do not have enough automaticity and word knowledge to figure things out.

It is critical that students catch the early word waves, for those who do will maintain an advantage through the later grades.

There Is a Difference Between Word Breadth and Word Depth

Words have glue—they carry a wide array of positive and negative connotations with them. Would you rather be hefty, muscular, or brawny? They all have similar meanings, but they all have different connotations. Owning all three of them gives you the power to select just the proper nuance in the context of your writing or speaking. Or take the word *plow*, for example. If you are a farmer in Kansas this word may evoke a different meaning than if you are a yoga instructor. A person who clears snow off highways may understand *plow* on a different level than a fullback on a football team. Having a broad vocabulary adds depth and nuance to your thinking.

Having strong word breadth can come into play when students are taking high-stakes assessments. The SAT, for example, often asks students questions similar to this:

> **In line 28, *engaged* most likely means**
>
> **A) involved**
>
> **B) interested**
>
> **C) busy**
>
> **D) captured**

Students need word breadth to answer this question correctly.

We also want students to gain word depth. You can know a word at the surface level, or you can know the same word at a deeper level. Take a word like *racism*, for example. I know what the word means, but as a white person who has lived a privileged life, I do not understand the word at the same level as someone who has been victimized.[7] The word evokes so much more than what's written on the page. Likewise, the word *comet* means something different to me than it does to an astrophysicist. I understand it on the surface level, but I don't *really* understand it. Or take the word *totalitarianism*—someone who lives in North Korea understands this word more than I do. And so on. Tom Newkirk said in a discussion about this chapter, "Prior knowledge of a word is not emotionally neutral. It is embedded in our emotional recollection. Take a word like *militia*, for example—in our society today, this word is fraught with danger." Our words are saturated with meaning, and our knowledge of them, as Willingham (2017) notes, "may be shallow, deep, or somewhere in between" (78).

An indication that students are achieving word depth is when they demonstrate flexibility in using words—for example, if they use *cut* as a noun ("I put a bandage on my cut.") and a verb ("He cut the paper."). Students also illustrate word depth when they can use a word that has multiple meanings, as shown in these sentences:

> Michelle caught a *bass* in the lake.
>
> Lindsay likes the *bass* player in Radiohead.

---

7. This is true of many isms (e.g., sexism, ageism, nepotism). People who have suffered from these have a deeper understanding of their meanings.

Katrina's bank account accumulated a lot of *interest*.

Taylor has an *interest* in manga.

Kalli took a *novel* approach to remodeling her home.

Robin's favorite *novel* to teach is *Fahrenheit 451*.

It is one thing to own a word. It is another to own it deeply, and, of course, gaining a deep understanding is often predicated on prior knowledge. The richer the prior knowledge, the more likely it is that deeper use of the word will occur.

When You Learn One Word, You Learn More Than One Word

At a conference I heard Shane Templeton, an author and a leading thinker on vocabulary development, say that if you learn one word, you are really learning many words. Take the word *help*, for example. Once you learn it, you are positioned to learn *helps*, *helped*, *helpful*, *helpless*, *unhelpful*, *helping*, *helper,* and *self-help.* Words are not learned one at a time. Learning one leads to exponential growth.

HOW TEACHERS CAN ADDRESS WORD POVERTY

Far and away, the best way to build vocabulary is through reading. Lots of it. But motivating young readers is harder than ever before—especially in a postpandemic, distraction-addicted world. So how do we motivate kids to read more? Let's start by looking at what *not* to do. In *Readicide* (2009), I offered this recipe for killing readers:

The Kill-a-Reader Casserole

Take one large novel. Dice into as many pieces as possible.

Douse with sticky notes.

Remove book from oven every five minutes and insert worksheets.

Add more sticky notes.

Baste until the novel is unrecognizable, far beyond well-done.

Serve in choppy, bite-size chunks. (73)

Let me flip this and offer suggestions on a recipe for building readers:

The Build-a-Reader Casserole

Collect the proper ingredients: lots of high-interest books across all genres.

Marinate the classroom with an enthusiasm for reading.

Sprinkle in daily book talks. Share what you are reading.

Mix in lots of choice. Balance the reading diet.

Knead in lots of independent reading.

Season with multiple book clubs.[1]

Bake into the schedule lots of time to read and to confer with kids.

Don't overcook with sticky notes, quizzes, worksheets, and packet work.

Not that many ingredients, but getting the mixture just right is difficult. Teachers have to find consistent funding for classroom libraries. They need to carve out time in the curriculum for kids to read and for teachers to confer. They have to coordinate and facilitate rich book club experiences. All of this while attending to the rest of the curriculum, the social-emotional needs of children (and sometimes colleagues), and all of the other responsibilities laid upon them. It's hard, which is why many books have been written on how to build readers (I recommend starting with Nancie Atwell and Anne Atwell Merkel's *The Reading Zone*, moving to Penny Kittle's *Book Love*, and then reading Donalyn Miller and Teri Lesesne's *The Joy of Reading*).

Over the years, I felt a great deal of stress in trying to get my students back into a reading groove. I knew what was at stake. I understood that strengthening their knowledge of words would be next to impossible if I couldn't move them from fake reading to real reading. And, of course, trying to motivate them was not just about strengthening their vocabularies. The more they read, the more they acquired knowledge. The more they acquired knowledge, the more they were likely to read. Readers who gain momentum benefit from the snowball effect.

Getting students to read is the first goal, but once that begins to occur, the focus shifts to three other goals that Penny Kittle and I established for young readers (Gallagher and Kittle 2018):

1. **Students will increase the complexity of reading.**
   Once reading momentum is established, we want students to move from "vacation" books to books where they will likely encounter more words that are

---

1. For in-depth thinking on how to set up and run student book clubs, see Chapter 2 of *4 Essential Studies*, a book I wrote with Penny Kittle (Kittle and Gallagher 2021).

unfamiliar. One of my favorite books is William Styron's *Sophie's Choice*. I can read it and follow the plot without a problem, but Styron challenges me with his vocabulary. In the first three pages alone I encountered *syllabic*, *alacrity*, *emolument*, *effrontery*, *magisterial*, *enervating*, and *supercilious*—and it's a 515-page novel! Likewise, I want kids to find books where they encounter unfamiliar words in context, which is unlikely to happen if they read only books that are too easy.

It has long been held that we should not give students material to read that is at their frustration level (frustration level is defined as less than 90 percent word accuracy), but Tim Shanahan, literacy expert and professor at the University of Illinois, challenges this notion. Shanahan argues that with proper teacher scaffolding, students can learn a lot from texts that many teachers may deem to be too hard (2015). When I taught *1984*, for example, I had to scaffold repeatedly so that my lower-ability readers could make sense of the novel. Some of my higher-ability readers got *1984* at an elevated level, and some of my lower-ability readers absorbed it at a lower level, but they all benefited from the experience. They could all discuss the dangers of language manipulation and government overreach. They could all connect it to what is happening in today's world. And since this chapter is about acquiring word knowledge, they were all exposed to numerous unfamiliar words in the context of the novel. These exposures undoubtedly grew their word banks.

Hard books are important for growth.[2] As I write this, I am reading Frank Wilczek's *Fundamentals: Ten Keys to Reality*. In this book, Wilczek, a Nobel laureate theoretical physicist, writes about the ideas that form our understanding of the universe—time, space, matter, energy, complexity, and complementarity. Wilczek tells the reader that he will write as simply as possible, but even so, there is much in the book I do not understand. But I am willing to live with this confusion because I am still learning a lot. I may not fully grasp the section on neutrinos, gravitons, and axions, but I'm only in Chapter 2 and I have already learned how GPS works, how we "see" stars that cannot be seen, and how archaeologists use carbon dating to determine the age of mummies. That's pretty cool.

While we want students to embrace hard reading, we must also be mindful that we kill readers when we ask them to read

2. Hard articles are also important for growth. Having students wrestle with difficult text at the article level proves helpful when we later ask them to read difficult books. In Chapter 4, we will look at the importance prior knowledge plays in reading shorter texts.

one hard book after another. The reading diet should be balanced, with room for vacation and just-right books as well.[3] This means lots of student choice. My students had partial or full choice on what they read over 80 percent of the time. I taught only one or two whole-class novels in a given year. This also means never starting the year by asking reluctant readers to read books that are very difficult. It is important to first reestablish reading identity and reading momentum before having them dive into a difficult core text.

We also must tread lightly when we say a book might be too easy or too hard for a student. Readability is often influenced by factors outside of the book, like prior knowledge and motivation. I am a reader, but I don't have one readability level. I have several. It depends on what I am reading. If you give me a book on surfing, I have high readability. If you give me a book on how to write computer code, I have low readability. Again, prior knowledge (a factor found outside the pages of the book) is a huge factor when determining a book's readability.

2. **Students will develop an allegiance to an author or a genre.**
Part of developing a reading identity is to find authors or genres (or both) that become yours. When these allegiances begin forming, students are not only more likely to read now but also more likely to read later.

One strong sign that kids are developing reading allegiances is when students get hooked on reading series. Children who read series books benefit in many ways: Their volume increases, thus leading to increased academic achievement. They are more likely to develop a love of reading and to share their enthusiasm for reading with others. They learn to read deeper, as many series delve into more complex characters and plots over time. And they gain confidence as one book builds upon another. Moving from one book in a series to the next creates a reading habit.

Of course, the younger readers are when they discover a series, the better. When my daughters were young, they went through a massive Goosebumps stage. They loved that series. Me? Not so much. But I remained patient, as I knew that these formulaic, morbid tales were helping my girls develop their identities as readers. I also knew that eventually they'd outgrow R. L. Stine's books and graduate to other series.

Many of my students, however, had never experienced this graduation. For years, I administered a survey during the first week of school and asked them to name their favorite authors and genres. Year in and year out, more than 90

3. Thanks to Nancie Atwell, who coined these terms.

percent of them could not do so. They had simply not developed allegiance to *any* author or genre. By the end of the year, I surveyed them again, with the hope that this had changed after spending a year with me.

3. **Students need to get into other reading lanes.**[4]
When it comes to word acquisition, we want to have students move beyond their favorite writer(s) and read more broadly. Someone who reads a lot of Stephen King will certainly benefit from the exposure to his broad vocabulary, but Stephen King's vocabulary is different from Jesmyn Ward's vocabulary. And Jesmyn Ward's vocabulary is different from Ocean Vuong's vocabulary. The more authors one reads, the broader the vocabulary exposure, and when this occurs, the broader the word acquisition will be.

Of course, there are other reasons we want students to read outside their initial reading lanes. Maybe most importantly, I want my students to read about people who are *unlike* them—those who come from different backgrounds, different regions of the country and world, and different points of view. Take Frankie, a former student of mine, for example. In a reading conference, I learned he was obsessed with NFL football. I also learned he hadn't really read an entire book in many years, so, naturally, I used his love of football as a hook. I pulled a number of books about professional football for him to consider, and he selected Clayton Geoffreys' *Patrick Mahomes*, a biography of the star Kansas City Chiefs quarterback. From there he read Michael Lewis' *The Blind Side* (he had seen the movie and liked it) before moving on to David Halberstam's *The Education of a Coach*, a profile of Bill Belichick, a future Hall of Fame coach. I then suggested *The League*, by John Eisenberg, which examines the origins of the NFL as we know it today.[5] Before Thanksgiving, Frankie—who hadn't read a book in years—had already read four books. His reading momentum had been reestablished.

But was that enough? The good news was that Frankie found himself in a reading lane again. The bad news was that Frankie was reluctant to get out of his football lane. If left alone, he would have read sports-related books all year. Staying in one reading lane would have restricted Frankie from acquiring a broader understanding of other people and places. It also would have narrowed his exposure to new vocabulary words. So I began nudging Frankie into broadening his reading.

---

4. I learned this goal from my friend Penny Kittle, who created it when we coauthored two books together.

5. The NFL was formed in a merger between rival leagues in 1966.

One way to ensure that students like Frankie get into other kinds of reading lanes is by building book club experiences. As I write this, I am consulting with the Anaheim Union High School District on creating reading experiences for grades seven through twelve. I am working with a team of teachers to select titles to anchor book club experiences around the theme of identity (see Figure 2–2).

These books expose students to many different worlds, from a story of gender fluidity (*The Prince and the Dressmaker*, grade seven) to an in-depth look at the legacy of slavery (*Stamped*, grade eleven). From a story about emigrating from war-torn Syria (*Other Words for Home*, grade eight) to a deep look at the injustices suffered by three generations of a family in rural Mississippi (*Sing, Unburied, Sing*, grade twelve). These books take students to different cultures (Korean, Mexican, Middle Eastern, and First Nation—in both the United States and Canada) and invite them to read about people who are unlike them.

We have chosen these books with the purpose of broadening our students' view of the world—to show them new and unfamiliar places and people. Positioning students to read outside their knowledge zones also builds empathy for others, inspires readers to learn new things, and expands prior knowledge. Broadening our students' reading pathways exposes them to even more new words, which is critical to building one's vocabulary bank.

When it comes to acquiring vocabularies, time spent reading clearly gets the biggest bang for the buck. One reason for this is that we are much more likely to learn words when we see them in context, as opposed to encountering them in isolation (Tulving and Gold 1963; Nation and Snowling 1998; Perfetti, Goldman, and Hogaboam 1979; Stanovich 1984). But there are other ways teachers can help their students broaden their vocabularies. Following are some of them.

Don't Fall into the Test-Prep Trap

In "Why American Students Haven't Gotten Better in Reading in 20 Years," Natalie Wexler (2020) discusses how curriculum is narrowed to prepare students for large-scale assessments and how this narrowing harms the development of young readers. (I also discuss this in greater detail in *Readicide* [2009].) Because schools are hell-bent on raising their reading and math scores, subjects such as history and science have often been placed on the back burner. (Wexler notes this is particularly an acute problem in high-poverty schools, and this narrowing often minimizes the curriculum

Seventh-Grade Theme: Who Am I?

The Way to Bea, by Kat Yeh
Front Desk, by Kelly Yang
Efrén Divided, by Ernesto Cisneros
The Prince and the Dressmaker, by Jen Wang
The Crossover, by Kwame Alexander

Eighth-Grade Theme: How Does One's Identity Change over Time?

Maybe He Just Likes You, by Barbara Dee
Other Words for Home, by Jasmine Warga
Miles Morales, by Brian Bendis
Speak (graphic novel), by Laurie Halse Anderson

Ninth-Grade Theme: How Is Our Identity Shaped by the People and Places We Know?

Piecing Me Together, by Renée Watson
Cemetery Boys, by Aiden Thomas
I Am Not Your Perfect Mexican Daughter, by Erika L. Sánchez
Boy21, by Matthew Quick
We Are Not from Here, by Jenny Torres Sanchez

Tenth-Grade Theme: How Does Our Identity Influence How We See Others?

The Poet X, by Elizabeth Acevedo
Patron Saints of Nothing, by Randy Ribay
You Should See Me in a Crown, by Leah Johnson
I Am Alfonso Jones, by Tony Medina
The Hate U Give, by Angie Thomas

Eleventh-Grade Theme: What Is the North American Experience?

Just Mercy, by Bryan Stevenson
Stamped, by Jason Reynolds and Ibram X. Kendi
Frankly in Love, by David Yoon
The Marrow Thieves, by Cherie Dimaline
Minor Feelings, by Cathy Park Hong

Twelfth-Grade Theme: How Do Your Choices Shape Your Identity? How Does Your Identity Shape Your Choices?

There There, by Tommy Orange
Sing, Unburied, Sing, by Jesmyn Ward
Educated, by Tara Westover
The Vanishing Half, by Brit Bennett
Little Fires Everywhere, by Celeste Ng

Figure 2–2

up to and through middle school.) When students learn less about history and science (and other subjects), their future in reading is hampered. If a student doesn't know anything about economics, she will have a hard time understanding a chapter on inflation.

Hirsch and Pondiscio, in "There Is No Such Thing as a Reading Test," give a concrete example of this. Think about a fourth-grade student, they say, in a struggling South Bronx elementary school sitting for a high-stakes exam:

> **The test begins, and the very first passage concerns the customs of the Dutch colony of New Amsterdam. You do not know what a custom is; neither do you know who the Dutch were, or even what a colony is. You have never heard of Amsterdam, old or new. Certainly it's never come up in class. Without background knowledge, you struggle with most of the passages on the test. You never had a chance. (2010)**

Hirsch and Pondiscio contrast this test-taking experience with that of students who come from more affluent backgrounds. They note that these students are not more capable, nor are they smarter. But because they sit down to take that test possessing wider general knowledge (as students from advantaged backgrounds often do), they are much more likely to perform better on the exam. *It's what they bring to the tests that elevates them.*

Narrowing the curriculum leads to a negative snowball effect—students who score low are funneled into a narrower curriculum so that they have extra time to work on their reading "skills." This creates a death spiral that *ensures* they will never catch up. Instead of narrowing the curriculum, we should be broadening our students' reading lives as much as possible. Every year, when my high school students were getting ready to take the SAT, I already knew who would score high on the verbal section. Almost without exception, it was those who had been reading for years.

There is a clear relationship between time spent reading and reading achievement (Samuels and Wu 2001; Whitten, Labby, and Sullivan 2016). If we want to prepare students for large-scale assessments, we need to widen the curriculum and do everything possible to get students to read more broadly. The added bonus to this approach? Students will build wider, more robust vocabularies.

Ditch the Weekly Vocabulary Lists

Giving students a list of vocabulary words to study each week is not good practice. Hirsch notes,

> **Spending large amounts of school time on individual word study is an inefficient and insufficient route to a bigger vocabulary. There are just too many words to be learned by 12th grade—between 25,000 and 60,000. A large vocabulary results not from memorizing word lists but from acquiring knowledge about the social and natural worlds. (2013)**

In a meta-analysis of numerous studies, Jeff McQuillan (2019) found that direct instruction of vocabulary lists was a poor approach to word acquisition. Instead, he found free reading "to be 1.7 times more efficient than direct instruction in building vocabulary in short-term treatments, and 12 times as efficient for long-term treatments." It is not through word study that we build broad vocabularies; it is through widespread reading.

My friend Cory, a nonreader, is learning this the hard way. He is preparing to take the GRE. He wants to become a physical therapist, which requires an advanced degree, but he is having trouble passing the practice tests. In one short passage that he read, he was confronted with three words he did not know: *garb*, *belied*, and *jejune*.[6] Yes, he could have studied vocabulary lists prior to the exam, but out of the thousands and thousands of possible words, what are the chances he would have studied (and remembered) these specific words? Highly unlikely. Let's just say there is a better chance the Angels will win this year's World Series. In other words, *highly* improbable. The current odds in Vegas for the Angels winning the World Series is 75:1. (Dear Arte Moreno, please sell the team.)

Teach Targeted Academic Vocabulary

Voluminous reading alone will not ensure that students acquire the vocabulary or academic language needed for success in content area classrooms. Sometimes, we need

6. A confession: I taught high school English for thirty-five years, I have a graduate degree, and this is the ninth book I have written, and I can honestly say that I am not aware of having ever seen the word *jejune*. This bugged me, so I asked five English teachers at my lunch table if they knew the definition. Not one of them knew the word. I'll save you the trouble: according to Dictionary.com, it's an adjective and it means "without interest or significance." Which raises another question: How does knowing this help one become a physical therapist?

to explicitly teach words. Take the concept of ecology, for example, which is taught in high school. The teacher will need to teach not only the word *ecology* but other words closely related to the concept. It is hard to understand *ecology* at a deep level without also knowing other terms such as *biodiversity*, *biomass*, *trophic levels*, *ecosystems*, *autotroph*, and *symbiosis*.

With this in mind, I suggest the following five proven strategies to help students acquire targeted academic vocabulary.

The Frayer Model

The Frayer Model is a graphic organizer (see Figure 2–3) created by Dorothy Frayer, Wayne Frederick, and Herbert Klausmeier at the University of Wisconsin in 1968. Students write the word to be learned in the center oval and then complete the outer boxes (which are self-explanatory). In Figure 2–3, Thuy, a tenth-grade student, is diving deep into the word *caucuses*. There are multiple variations of this model as well—a quick internet search will lead you to numerous adaptations.

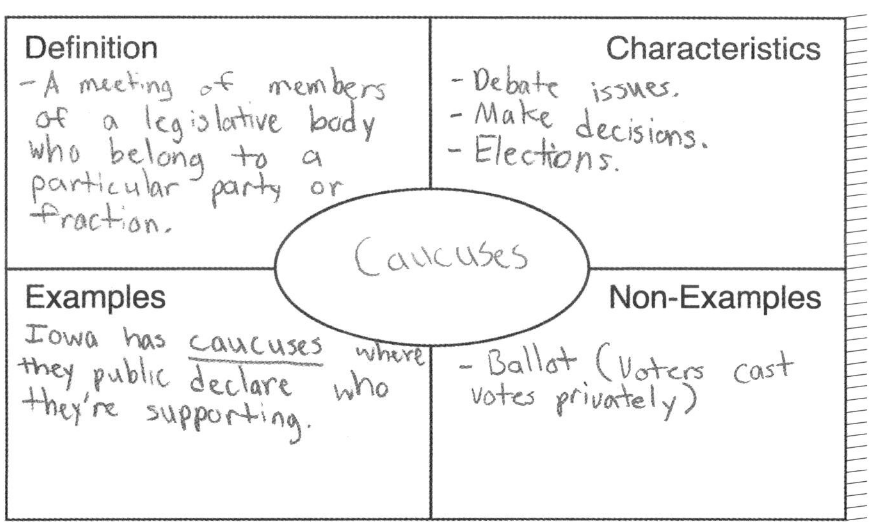

Figure 2–3

A word chart

Created by Larry Ferlazzo and Katie Hull-Sypnieski in *The ELL Teacher's Toolbox: Hundreds of Practical Ideas to Support Your Students*, the word chart (Figure 2–4) is tailored to helping English language learners (2018, 30).

Paragraph Number	Word	Definition in English Using My Own Words	Definition in Home Language and/or Picture	My Own Sentence

Figure 2–4

Vocabulary illustrations

In *Word Nerds*, Brenda J. Overturf, Leslie H. Montgomery, and Margot Holmes Smith (2013, 83) recommend having students draw illustrations to represent new words. In Figure 2–5 you will see how Nanjibo, an English language learner, uses art to comprehend unfamiliar words found in *Romeo and Juliet*.

Figure 2–5

A variation of this activity would be to have students cut and paste digital images under each of the words.

Word predictions

This approach to learning new words, which I learned from Elfrieda "Freddy" Hiebert,[7] begins by having students see the word in context in two different sentences (see Figure 2–6). This pairing of sentences adds a richer level of context that helps students predict the meaning of the word. Once students make their predictions, the teacher gives them a nondictionary definition of the word and asks them to brainstorm related words. Last, the teacher gives students the word in different languages. In the example in Figure 2–6, the words have been translated into Spanish, Arabic, and Vietnamese—the languages most spoken by the ELL students at my former school.

Word	Word in Context	Predicted Meaning	Actual Meaning	Related Words	Other Languages
concede	While I lost one battle, I wasn't about to **concede** the war. In the middle of an argument, most people will **concede** that the other person has a good point.				conceder công nhận tatanazal
acknowledge	She looked the other way and refused to **acknowledge** what I said. It shows character to **acknowledge** your mistakes.				admitir thừa nhận yuqr

Figure 2–6

(continues)

7. Freddy is one of this nation's top experts on vocabulary. She sat next to me and sketched out this chart. To go deeper, I recommend her book *Teaching Words and How They Work: Small Changes for Big Vocabulary Results* (2019).

Word	Word in Context	Predicted Meaning	Actual Meaning	Related Words	Other Languages
gauntlet	He was always willing to take up the **gauntlet** for a good cause. The **gauntlet** had been thrown down: only five players will make the team.				guante alqufaaz găng tay

Figure 2–6 *Continued*

Cheat sheet

Before reading, the teacher selects some key terms and provides students with non-dictionary definitions, as I did in Figure 2–7. In framing Chapter 1 of *Dr. Jekyll and Mr. Hyde*, for example, I said, "Here are four words that will help you better understand this chapter. Let's review them before reading."

The students did not spend valuable class time looking up the meaning of these words. The definitions were provided for them. They then kept this cheat sheet alongside the text as they read.[8]

If you teach in a school where students are subjected to a lot of standardized testing, you might also consider teaching keywords associated with these exams. There are many lists available online, but you might start with this list: *analyze*, *persuade*, *compare*, *contrast*, *summarize*, *demonstrate*, *describe*, *interpret*, *explain*, and *infer*. You can teach these words using any of the aforementioned strategies in this section.

8. Of course, selecting which words to preview is a crapshoot, as students come to the text with varying degrees of vocabulary knowledge.

Dr. Jekyll and Mr. Hyde Chapter 1 Vocabulary Preview	
Word	**Nondictionary Definition**
countenance (n.)	Appearance of the face. **Example:** *He had a worried countenance after realizing he lost his wallet.*
austere (adj.)	Strict, forbidding, uncompromising. **Example:** *She was an austere teacher. No joking was allowed.*
sawbones (n.)	A surgeon. **Example:** *They called for the sawbones immediately to fix the broken leg.*
reprove (v.)	To correct. **Example:** *The teacher reproved the student for the spelling error.*

Figure 2–7

Teach Readers to Be Active When Faced with an Unfamiliar Word

So, what should a reader do when encountering an unfamiliar word? I wanted my readers to be active, not passive. When they didn't know a word, I wanted them to *do something*. Following are some actions students might take.

Attack the word

To teach students word-attack skills, I grouped students and asked them if they could figure out the meaning of the following word:

pneumonoultramicroscopicsilicovolcanoconiosis[9]

This activity teaches students to pay close attention to word parts (e.g., *pneumono* refers to the lungs; *micro* means small).

9. Yes, this is a real word. *Pneumono* refers to the lung. *Ultra* means extremely. *Microscopic* means tiny. *Silico* is sand. *Volcano* is self-evident. *Coniosis* is scarring. Put them all together and you have a lung disease caused by breathing volcanic dust. You also have the longest word in the English language.

Once students understood they could break words down, I introduced the 30-15-10 list to them (see Figure 2–8). This chart, which I initially shared in *Deeper Reading* (2004, 72–73), contains the thirty most common prefixes, the fifteen most common roots, and the ten most common suffixes. (This chart is also available as an online resource.)

The 30-15-10 List
The most common prefixes, roots, and suffixes

Prefix	Meaning	Example
a, ab, abs	away, from	absent, abstinence
ad, a, ac, af, ag, an, ar, at, as	to, toward	adhere, annex, accede, adapt
bi, bis	two	bicycle, biped, bisect
circum	around	circumference
com, con	together, with	combination, connect
de	opposite, from, away	detract, defer, demerit
dis, dif, di	apart, not	disperse, different
epi	upon, on top of	epicenter
equi	equal	equality, equitable
ex, e	out, from, forth	eject, exhale, exit
hyper	over, above	hyperactive, hypersensitive
hypo	under, beneath	hypodermic
in, en	in, into, not	inject, endure, incorrect
inter	between, among	intercede
mal, male	bad, ill	malpractice, malevolent
mis	wrong	mistake, misunderstand
mono	alone, single, one	monotone, monopoly
non	not	nonsense
ob	in front of, against	obstacle
omni	everywhere, all	omnipresent
preter	past, beyond	preternatural

Figure 2–8

Prefix	Meaning	Example
pro	forward	proceed, promote
re	again, back	recall, recede
retro	backward, behind, back	retroactive
se	apart	secede
sub	under	subway
super	greater, beyond	supernatural, superstition
trans	across, beyond	transcend, transcontinental
un, uni	one	unilateral, unity
un (pronounced uhn)	not	unhappy, unethical
Root	**Meaning**	**Example**
bas	low	basement
cap, capt	take, seize	capture, capable
cred	believe	credible
dict	speak	predict, dictionary
duc, duct	lead	induce, conduct
fac, fact	make, do	artifact, facsimile
graph	write	autograph, graphic
log	word, study of	dialogue, biology
mort	die, death	mortal, mortician
scrib, script	write	transcribe, subscription
spec, spect	see	specimen, aspect
tact	touch	contact, tactile
ten	hold	tenacious, retentive
therm	heat	thermostat, thermometer
ver	true	verify
Suffix	**Meaning**	**Example**
able, ible	able to (adj.)	usable
er, or	one who does (n.)	competitor

Figure 2–8 *Continued*

(*continues*)

Suffix	Meaning	Example
fy	to make (v.)	dignify
ism	the practice of (n.)	rationalism, Catholicism
ist	one who is occupied with (n.)	feminist, environmentalist
less	without, lacking (adj.)	meaningless
logue, log	a particular kind of speaking or writing (n.)	prologue, dialogue
ness	the quality of (n.)	aggressiveness
ship	the art or skill of (n.)	sportsmanship
tude	the state of (n.)	gratitude

Figure 2–8 *Continued*

I had students learn these ten at a time, and I quizzed them on them. The first week they were responsible for the first ten, the second week they were responsible for the first ten again plus the next ten, and so on.

As students were learning these over the course of six weeks, I often picked a word of the day and asked students to wrestle with it (e.g., "What does *unenviable* mean?").

Look at the context

To help my students understand how context clues can help us derive meaning, I gave them a sentence with a nonsense word in it and asked them to answer one question:

> The comic was *bloog*; the audience was roaring in laughter.
> *Bloog* most likely means
>
> A) depressing
> B) interesting
> C) hilarious
> D) funny

Most of my students were able to answer correctly. I liked using a nonsense word because it sent the message that a reader could learn a word she had never seen before. I was also sure to create nonsense words that could not be broken down by word parts—again, this accentuated the importance of context.

Another way to teach context clues is to give students sentences with a word missing and ask them to predict the missing word. Here, for example, are the first lines of various books, all with a missing word:

> Montgomery Hughes ________ his duffel bag shut and scanned his bedroom one more time. (Dustin Grinnell, *The Empathy Academy*, 2020, 3)
>
> A boy is coming down a ________ of stairs. (Maggie O'Farrell, *Hamnet*, 2021, 4)
>
> My suffering left me sad and ________. (Yann Martel, *Life of Pi*, 2003, 3)
>
> I was driving a Lexus through a ________ wind. (Don DeLillo, *Underworld*, 2015, 6)
>
> The sky above the Mississippi River stretched out like a ________. (Clint Smith, *How the Word Is Passed*, 2022, 3)
>
> Answers in sequence: zipped, flight, gloomy, rustling, song

As shown in these examples, I suggest starting out with sentences that are easier to guess and then progressing to ones that are more difficult. This helps students build their knowledge of synonyms as well.

Decide their reading is good enough and move on

When reading just-right or challenge books, it is likely you'll encounter many unfamiliar words. If you stopped at every word you did not know, the act of reading would become overly burdensome. The key is to develop a sense of when you should stop and when it is OK to keep moving. Take this sentence from Frank Wilczek's *Fundamentals: Ten Keys to Reality*, for example:

> **Knowing the size of Earth's orbit around the Sun, we can use it to determine the distance to some relatively nearby stars directly, using Euclidean geometry. (2022, 24)**

Here was my thought process as I read that sentence: *What? There are different types of geometry? How did I not know this? What other kinds of geometry are there besides Euclidean?*[10] *Do I specifically need to know the difference between Euclidean geometry and other types of geometry to understand this sentence? I don't think so. Move along.*

---

10. Apparently, there are several types: non-Euclidean, analytic, differential, hyperbolic, elliptical. One type—the type I learned in high school—was enough for me, thank you. Whatever that type was.

Now contrast that thinking with the thinking I had when I read the following sentence from the same book:

> **By careful study of Cepheid variables in the Magellanic Clouds, Henrietta Leavitt (1868–1921) established that Cepheid variables that pulsate at the same rate also have the same brightness, and so provide standard candles. (27)**

There is no way I can comprehend this sentence without knowing what a Cepheid variable is, and I'm likely going to need to know what Magellanic Clouds are as well.[11] *Clearly, my reading is not good enough to simply gloss over these unfamiliar words, and using word-attack skills is not going to be helpful here. Time to look up some words.*

Read next to their phone

I often read with my phone next to me so I can look up any critical unknown words. Again, I stop only if I have determined that the unknown word is essential. The Dictionary.com app is one of my most frequently used apps, and I encourage students to use this or similar tools. One important caveat that I tell students: If you are going to use your phone while you read, turn your notifications off. Really.

Build a Love of Words

I love words, and I want to build a culture in which students love them as well. Here are some ways I have celebrated words in my classroom.

List of words I like and don't like

In my notebook, I keep a list of words I like and words I do not like (see Figure 2–9). As students read their independent books, core works, and book club selections throughout the school year, have them generate their own lists of words in their notebooks.

Favorite word or least-favorite word

Each student identifies a favorite word and writes a one-page informational piece. They may address some or all of the following: Why is this word your favorite? Is there

11. A Cepheid variable "is a variable star in which changes in brightness are due to alternate contractions and expansions in volume." A Magellanic Cloud is "either of two irregular clusters in the southern heavens that are the nearest independent star system to the Milky Way." (Both definitions courtesy of Dictionary.com.)

Words I Like	Words I Do Not Like
blunt	Arte Moreno
bodacious	bad
brouhaha	cancer
discombobulated	chafe
doofus	clogged
doohickey	clot
feckless	cramp
flabbergasted	curd
flummoxed	diarrhea
heft	designated hitter
hoodwink	fester
hummus	glioblastoma
igloo	influencer
jalopy	jury duty
jetty	like
lickspittle	literally
lollygag	mucus
melancholy	no problem
moot	phlegm
nostril	pus
obloquy	regurgitate
palimpsest	secrete
solipsistic	selfie
torpid	spasm
trombone	tax
turgid	very
vapid	vomit
willy-nilly	whatever
wombat	wretch

Figure 2–9

a story tied to this word? What is the derivation of the word? What is your history with this word? Or, conversely, students may create one-minute videos explaining their least-favorite words. As a mentor text, I used Matthew McConaughey's (2022) short "Least Favorite Word" video (found on YouTube), where he discusses his disdain for the word *unbelievable*. Of course, students can do either approach as a digital, rather than a written, text.

Word of the day

When students walked into class, I sometimes had a word of the day (and its definition) on the document camera for all to see. I didn't often refer to it—it was just there as a daily reminder that words are cool, something to ponder before class started. No note-taking. No quizzes. Just fifteen seconds of word appreciation. One of my favorite sources for these unusual words is Susie Dent's X (formerly Twitter) account (@susie_dent), where today I learned that *woofits* means a sense of unease or a case of the blahs. I did not expect my students to remember these words—it was just an exercise in building appreciation of the wonders of the English language.

Occasionally, with older students, I've mixed in a week or two of words that sound dirty but are not. Here are five of them:

> *aholehole* (pronounced ah-holy-holy): a fish found in Hawaii
>
> *bumfiddler:* a person who pollutes or spoils something
>
> *humpenscrump:* a crudely made musical instrument
>
> *lollpoop:* a lazy, ineffectual individual who always gets to a task just as someone else has finished it
>
> *sexagesm:* one-sixtieth of something (Jones 2019)

Another variation of word of the day is to introduce students to Rich Hall's (1984) *sniglets*. A sniglet is a word that doesn't appear in the dictionary but should. For example, here are two of Hall's humorous made-up words:

> *aquadextrous:* possessing the ability to turn the bathtub faucet on and off with your toes (10).
>
> *optortionist:* the kid in school who can turn his eyelids inside out (57).

Sometimes I introduced the word and had students guess the definition. Once they got the feel of sniglets, I invited them to create their own.

CLOSING THOUGHTS

Knowing words begins with the ability to decode them, and for young readers, Taft and Leslie (1985) found that topic knowledge positively influenced word identification. Additionally, Priebe, Keenan, and Miller (2011) found children with better decoding skills are also often those who have a wide range of prior knowledge. The researchers found "that it is quite easy to find poor readers who do not have prior knowledge of assorted passage topics; however, it is much harder to find good readers who do not have prior knowledge. Better word decoding skill appears to go hand in hand with an increased chance of having prior knowledge."

Knowing more words comes with huge benefits: owning words makes you smarter, which, in turn, enables you to more easily connect with new learning. Prior knowledge is the foundation of comprehension, and comprehension starts with knowing words. Lots of them.

The US military understands this. Since the 1950s, it has administered the Armed Forces Qualification Test (AFQT) to help determine job allocation for those entering service. Hirsch (2013) notes,

> **The exam consists of two verbal sections (on vocabulary size and paragraph comprehension) and two math sections. The military has determined that the test predicts real-world job performance most accurately when you *double* the verbal score and add it to the math score. (italics mine)**

This bears repeating: the best predictor of real-world job performance comes when the participants' verbal score is doubled. Hirsch also notes that a student's verbal score accurately predicts future income as well.

Judith Cofer was right: words are weapons and tools. If we are to adequately arm our students, we must do all we can to lift them out of word poverty. We must not forget there is a strong correlation between vocabulary knowledge and reading comprehension. You have to know stuff to read stuff, and knowing stuff starts with knowing words, words, words.[12]

WORKS CITED

Dale, Edgar. 1965. "Vocabulary Measurement: Techniques and Major Findings." *Elementary English* 42 (8): 898.

DeLillo, Don. 1997. *Underworld.* New York: Scribner.

Ferlazzo, Larry, and Katie Hull-Sypnieski. 2018. *The ELL Teacher's Toolbox: Hundreds of Practical Ideas to Support Your Students.* San Francisco: Jossey-Bass.

12. And not knowing many words may bring on a case of the woofits.

Frayer, Dorothy Ann, Wayne C. Frederick, and Herbert J. Klausmeier. 1969. *A Schema for Testing the Level of Concept Mastery: Report from the Project on Situational Variables and Efficiency of Concept Learning. Madison, WI: Wisconsin Research and Development Center for Cognitive Learning.* http://www.worldcat.org/title/schema-for-testing-the-level-of-concept-mastery-report-from-the-project-on-situational-variables-and-efficiency-of-concept-learning/oclc/5085175.

Gallagher, Kelly. 2004. *Deeper Reading: Comprehending Challenging Texts, 4–12*. Portsmouth, NH: Stenhouse.

———. 2009. *Readicide: How Schools Are Killing Reading and What You Can Do About It*. Portland, ME: Stenhouse.

Gallagher, Kelly, and Penny Kittle. 2018. *180 Days: Two Teachers and the Quest to Engage and Empower Adolescents*. Portsmouth, NH: Heinemann.

Grinnell, Dustin. 2022. *Empathy Academy*. Austin, TX: Atmosphere.

Hall, Rich. 1984. *Sniglets*. New York: Macmillan.

Hart, Betty, and Todd R. Risley. 1995. *Meaningful Differences in the Everyday Experience of Young American Children*. Baltimore, MD: Paul H. Brookes.

Heingartner, Douglas. 2020. "Americans' Vocabulary Skills Are Dropping, Despite the Growing Percentage of College Graduates." SuchScience. August 18. https://suchscience.org/why-are-americans-vocabulary-skills-stagnating/.

Hiebert, Elfrieda. 2019. *Teaching Words and How They Work: Small Changes for Big Vocabulary Results*. New York: Teachers College Press.

Hirsch, E. D., Jr. 2013. "A Wealth of Words." *City Journal* (Winter). https://www.city-journal.org/html/wealth-words-13523.html.

Hirsch, E. D., Jr., and Robert Pondiscio. 2010. "There's No Such Thing as a Reading Test." *The American Prospect*, June 14. https://prospect.org/special-report/thing-reading-test/.

Jones, Paul Anthony. 2023. "50 Words That Sound Dirty but Actually Aren't." Mental Floss. Sept.13. https://www.mentalfloss.com/article/58036/50-words-sound-rude-actually-arent.

Kittle, Penny, and Kelly Gallagher. 2021. *4 Essential Studies: Beliefs and Practices to Reclaim Student Agency*. Portsmouth, NH: Heinemann.

Lemoine, Hope E., Betty A. Levy, and Ann Hutchinson. 1993. "Increasing the Naming Speed of Poor Readers: Representations Formed Across Repetitions." *Journal of Experimental Child Psychology* 55 (3): 297–328. https://doi.org/10.1006/jecp.1993.1018.

Martel, Yann. 2003. *Life of Pi*. Edinburgh, Scotland: Canongate.

McConaughey, Matthew. 2022. "Matthew McConaughey's Least Favorite Word." Matthew McConaughey, May 16. YouTube video, 0:56. https://www.youtube.com/watch?v=034I6sw-oYU.

McKeown, Margaret G., Isabel L. Beck, Richard C. Omanson, and Martha T. Pople. 1985. "Some Effects of the Nature and Frequency of Vocabulary Instruction on the Knowledge and Use of Words." *Reading Research Quarterly* 20 (5): 522–35.

McQuillan, Jeff. 2019. "The Inefficiency of Vocabulary Instruction." *International Electronic Journal of Elementary Education* 11 (4): 309–18. https://files.eric.ed.gov/fulltext/EJ1212396.pdf.

Nation, Kate, and Margaret J. Snowling. 1998. "Individual Differences in Contextual Facilitation: Evidence from Dyslexia and Poor Reading Comprehension." *Child Development* 69 (4): 996–1011.

O'Farrell, Maggie. 2021. *Hamnet: A Novel of the Plague*. New York: Knopf.

Orwell, George. 1949. *1984*. New York: Harcourt Brace.

Otsuka, Julie. 2022. *The Swimmers*. New York: Knopf.

Overturf, Brenda J., Leslie H. Montgomery, and Margot Holmes Smith. 2013. *Word Nerds: Teaching All Students to Learn and Love Vocabulary*. Portland, ME: Stenhouse.

Perfetti, Charles A., Susan R. Goldman, and Thomas W. Hogaboam. 1979. "Reading Skill and the Identification of Words in Discourse Context." *Memory and Cognition* 7 (4): 273–82.

Priebe, Sarah J., Janice M. Keenan, and Amanda C. Miller. 2011. "How Prior Knowledge Affects Word Identification and Comprehension." *Reading and Writing* 7: 581–86. https://www.ncbi.nlm.nih.gov/pmc/articles/PMC3142886/.

Rosenblatt, Louise M. 1970. *Literature as Exploration*. New York: Random House.

Samuels, Stanley Jay, and Yi-Chen Wu. 2001. *How the Amount of Time Spent on Independent Reading Affects Reading Achievement: A Response to the National Reading Panel*. CiteSeerX. https://citeseerx.ist.psu.edu/document?repid=rep1&type=pdf&doi=ce1f459adbbae5978d07378bd5611e045efd4f04.

Scholastic. 2019. "Kids and Family Reading Report." https://www.scholastic.com/readingreport/navigate-the-world.html.

Shanahan, Timothy. 2016. "How Many Times Should They Copy the Spelling Words?" *Shanahan on Literacy* (blog), March 6. https://www.shanahanonliteracy.com/blog/how-many-times-should-they-copy-the-spelling-words#sthash.KXVMEtZG.dpbs.

———. 2015. "More on the Instructional Level and Challenging Text." *Shanahan on Literacy* (blog), August 30. http://www.shanahanonliteracy.com/blog/more-on-the-instructional-level-and-challenging-text.

Smith, Clint. 2022. *How the Word Is Passed: A Reckoning with the History of Slavery Across America*. New York: Little, Brown.

Stanovich, Keith E. 1984. "The Interactive-Compensatory Model of Reading: A Confluence of Developmental, Experimental, and Educational Psychology." *RASE: Remedial and Special Education* 5 (3): 11–19.

Taft, Mary L., and Lauren Leslie. 1985. "The Effects of Prior Knowledge and Oral Reading Accuracy on Miscues and Comprehension." *Journal of Reading Behavior* 17 (2): 163–79.

Tulving, Endel, and Cecille Gold. 1963. "Stimulus Information and Contextual Information as Determinants of Tachistoscopic Recognition of Words." *Journal of Experimental Psychology* 66 (4): 319–27.

Wexler, Natalie. 2018. "Why American Students Haven't Gotten Better at Reading in 20 Years." *The Atlantic*, May 18. https://www.theatlantic.com/education/archive/2018/04/-american-students-reading/557915/.

Whitten, Christy, Sandra Labby, and Sam L. Sullivan. 2016. "The Impact of Pleasure Reading on Academic Success." *Journal of Multidisciplinary Graduate Research* 2: 48–64. https://jmgr-ojs-shsu.tdl.org/jmgr/index.php/jmgr/article/view/11.

Wilczek, Frank. 2022. *Fundamentals: Ten Keys to Reality*. New York: Penguin Books.

Williams, Conor P. 2020. "New Research Ignites Debate on the '30 Million Word Gap.'" Edutopia. October 13. https://www.edutopia.org/article/new-research-ignites-debate-30-million-word-gap.

Willingham, Daniel T. 2017. *The Reading Mind: A Cognitive Approach to Understanding How the Mind Reads*. San Francisco: Jossey-Bass.

The more
you know,
the better
you read.

The Importance of Prior Knowledge AT THE SENTENCE AND PASSAGE LEVELS

In trying to comprehend a sentence, there are two types of prior knowledge that come into play: syntactic cues and the general knowledge we bring to the page. Let's look at each.

UNDERSTANDING SYNTACTIC CUES

Take this sentence from George Saunders' *A Swim in a Pond in the Rain*, for example:

> **We live, as you may have noticed, in a degraded era, bombarded by facile, shallow, agenda-laced, too rapidly disseminated information bursts. (2021, 5)**

Figure 3–1 shows how my thinking went when I read this sentence.

I ran into a bit of confusion at the end of the sentence. Is the word *information* the last in the series of five adjectives describing the *bursts*? Or is *information bursts* one thing—a compound noun that follows four adjectives? I had to read the sentence twice, relying on my previous syntactic knowledge to make sense of it.

There are other clues that readers pick up on as well. Consider this sentence:

> **First, MLB has implemented a pitch clock, and it has worked to shorten games.**

You know that when you encounter the word *and* in the center of the sentence, it will be followed by something that adds to the first half of the sentence. And because the sentence begins with *First,* you can anticipate that other items in a list will follow later in the paragraph. As Wexler notes, "if students are unfamiliar with a grammatical concept like a subordinating conjunction, they may be stymied by a sentence using that structure, even if they're fluent decoders and have adequate vocabularies" (2023).

We can discern the difference between experienced and inexperienced student writers by simply looking at their syntax. Inexperienced writers lack rhythm in their writing because they often stack one simple sentence on top of another. Experienced writers, on the other hand, unconsciously "rely on a stock of established moves that

What I Read	What I Thought as I Read
We live,	He is going to describe where we live, but because the comma immediately follows the verb, I suspect a brief diversion is coming.
as you may have noticed,	This is an aside—an interrupter—he will soon come back to his main point of where we live.
in a degraded era,	This is where we live, but again, the comma tells me additional information is coming, probably to say more about this degraded era.
bombarded by facile, shallow, agenda-laced, too rapidly disseminated information bursts.	These are all adjectives, as they come before what they are describing.

Figure 3–1

are crucial for communicating sophisticated ideas" (Graff and Birkenstein 2006, 1). Noted educator and researcher Francis Christensen says, "We think naturally in primer sentences, progress naturally to compound sentences, and must be taught to combine the primer sentences into complex sentences—and that complex sentences are the mark of maturity" (1963, 155).

In *They Say / I Say: The Moves That Matter in Academic Writing*, Graff and Birkenstein ask us to think about activities we know how to do particularly well, like playing the piano, shooting a basketball, or driving a car (2006, 1). Once we have mastered this skill, we give very little conscious thought to the steps involved in doing it. "Performing this activity . . . depends on you having learned a series of complicated moves—moves that may seem mysterious or difficult to those who haven't learned them" (1).

Experienced writers (and readers) have mastered a number of writerly moves, while inexperienced writers often lack any rhythm to their writing. To illustrate this, let's look at a passage written by one of my twelfth-grade students, Julianna:

> **America has always been a safe haven and advocate for prosperity and growth. What happens when America has grown too much? Overcrowding in other countries is not unheard of. Places like China have 1.442 billion people living on top of each other. It's a fight for space. Our epidemic of too many people living together has grown. This continual expansion of population, may result in a regulated policies that might have controversial effects. This will cut short our "natural rights" as citizens. Others might say we should just "build more apartments," to fit the growing population.**

Notice there is no sentence branching here. It's just one simple sentence stacked upon another. She does use two commas, but uses both incorrectly, and it is unclear whom she is quoting in the final two sentences.

For contrast, here is a passage written by Zaira, a student in the same class:

> **In the United States, a teenager is officially labeled as an adult at the age of 18. A teenager who turns 18 is confronted with responsibilities: being employed, paying the phone bill, driving a vehicle. Nonetheless, I know a number of teenagers younger than 18 who have moved out from home and are forced to live on their own. The government will argue that there is a reason why there**

should be a legal age for adulthood because there needs to be an average age of maturity. However, age doesn't determine whether a person has become an adult. A teenager who begins to work at the age of 16, attends school, takes care of her siblings, and sustains the household with more than half of their paycheck—this is an actual representation of a responsible individual.

Notice that Zaira possesses a set of writerly moves that Julianna does not have, such as the following techniques:

- She uses dependent clauses to start sentences (*Nonetheless* and *However*).
- She uses the word *however* to signify that she is going to offer a counterpoint.
- She uses a colon to precede a list.
- She writes items in a series that lead to a dash, followed by her thesis statement.
- She employs strategic repetition: *teenager*, *adult*, and *adulthood*.

These are sophisticated sentence-level moves—moves that Graff and Birkenstein (2006) argue should be taught. For example, in opening a debate, the authors suggest that the following template is useful:

In discussions of X, one controversial issue has been __________________. On the one hand, __________________ argues ______________________________________. On the other hand, __________________________ contends ______________________________. Others even maintain ____________________________. My own view is __________________________. (24)

This template nudges inexperienced writers to begin sentences with dependent clauses (*On the one hand*), helping them break out of the monotony of one simple sentence followed by another. Once students begin to adopt these moves, the hope is that they will internalize them to the point where they use them unconsciously. This will happen only, of course, if students are reading and writing regularly.

For an example, let's return to Zaira's passage and look at her first sentence: "In the United States, a teenager is officially labeled as an adult at the age of 18." When reading this, we immediately get the sense that the writer thinks there is something wrong with this assumption, and we anticipate that a pushback is coming. She is applying this move: "It is generally understood that ____________, but ______________." We can sense that a counterpoint is coming even before we see the word *However*. Zaira has unconsciously adopted this writing move, which makes it a lot easier for her to read writers who use this move.

BRINGING GENERAL KNOWLEDGE TO THE PAGE

Beyond the syntactic and morphological knowledge we bring to a sentence, we also rely on general knowledge to make sense of sentences. When I read the sentence about the pitch clock—"First, MLB has implemented a pitch clock, and it has worked to shorten games"—I tapped in to the following knowledge:

- *MLB* is an abbreviation for *Major League Baseball*.
- A pitch clock means that pitchers will have fifteen seconds to pitch the ball when there is not a runner on base.
- They will get eighteen seconds when there is a base runner.
- The batter will need to be in the batter's box before the pitch clock gets to eight seconds.
- Violators will be penalized. Pitchers will be awarded a ball. Batters will be awarded a strike.
- This change was first tried in the minor leagues, and it worked—games were shortened an average of twenty-five minutes.
- Many pitchers came out against this change.

My deep understanding of the sentence was possible because I possess all the essential elements of prior knowledge, as evidenced in this equation:

> **word knowledge + syntactic knowledge + background knowledge = deep understanding**

INTRODUCING PRIOR KNOWLEDGE AT THE SENTENCE LEVEL

When introducing the importance of prior knowledge to students, I started at the sentence level. Here are some types of one-sentence micropractice sources.

Cartoons

Start with a cartoon like the one in Figure 3–2, from Dan Misdea (2023) in the *New Yorker*.

Have students list what they would need to know to fully understand this cartoon:

- what a sloth looks like
- that sloths are known to move very slowly
- that March Madness refers to the college basketball tournament to determine a national champion
- that teams are placed in a sixty-four-team bracket

"Don't even bother—we missed the deadline to finish our March Madness brackets again."

Figure 3–2

Political Cartoons

Select a political cartoon for which students will likely lack the necessary prior knowledge, like the one from Pat Bagley (2022) in Figure 3–3.

Many students can read the sentence in the cartoon, but they do not understand it. Their lack of comprehension is not due to a fluency problem. It is not related to a deficiency in phonemic awareness. It stems from a lack of prior knowledge. If they do not know Mike Lee,[1] they have zero chance of understanding the cartoon. It would also help to know that an elephant is a symbol for the Republican Party and that a pledge is foundational to being a Boy Scout.

Figure 3–3

Memes

Students enjoy analyzing memes. Some of my favorites involve martial artist and actor Chuck Norris. Years ago, a "No one is tougher than Chuck Norris" fad began, which highlighted humorous and absurd feats of strength and endurance. Here are two of my favorites:

> Chuck Norris does not use spell check. If he happens to misspell a word, Oxford will change the spelling.
>
> Chuck Norris is the reason Waldo is hiding. (Miller 2023)

A reader would need to know Oxford and Waldo to understand these memes. Other Chuck Norris memes can be found via a simple online search. Have students select one and identify the prior knowledge they would need to understand the meme.

Tweets

When the cryptocurrency FTX collapsed, authorities in the Bahamas raided the FTX company offices. This created a flurry of tweets on X (formerly Twitter) about the situation. To understand these various threads, you'd have to know the following:

- FTX is a cryptocurrency platform.
- Over one million people invested in FTX. Their money disappeared in a matter of hours when the currency crashed.

1. Mike Lee is a senator from Utah. In 2022, he reneged on his 2010 promise to serve only two terms. He was then reelected for a third term.

- The Bahamas is a tax haven that doesn't always comply with international tax standards. The country has no personal, capital gains, estate gift, or inheritance taxes. It also doesn't have corporate tax, unless that revenue is derived inside the country. (Ramkumar 2022)
- The Bahamas regulatory oversight is more lax than regulations found in the United States. (Ramkumar 2022)
- Sam Bankman was arrested and convicted of fraud.

In the threads, there was speculation about the company's ties to Russia and its war in Ukraine, to possible CIA involvement, and to politicians who may have benefitted from inside information. Because my background knowledge of cryptocurrency and how it works is sketchy at best, I lack the background knowledge necessary to make sense of it all.

One last way to teach students the importance prior knowledge plays in understanding at the sentence level is to have them find and respond to what I call pushback sentences. These are sentences that a reader who possesses prior knowledge can challenge, or push back against. For example, take this sentence:

> **Studies show that students are not getting enough sleep; therefore, the beginning of the school day should be moved up.**

As a reader, I possess enough prior knowledge to push back against this sentence. Yes, it is true that many students come to school sleep deprived. It is also true that academic performance improves when students are better rested. But my experience in California—the first state to mandate that high school classes cannot start earlier than eight thirty—is that a later start time became an invitation for high school students to stay up even later the night before. This is not simply my observation. I polled a group of teachers, who felt the same way. They told me that students did not appear better rested and that attendance did not improve. The first-period tardy problem, they said, got *worse* after the law passed. Many parents now leave for work before their students go to school, and because of this, they are not there to nudge their adolescents out the door.

Have students find pushback sentences by reading an online newspaper. They can select sentences in any area of the newspaper—politics, sports, or the arts—and then explain why the sentences they have selected may not be giving the full picture. This activity builds inference skills and teaches them the value of prior knowledge.

HOW TO HELP READERS BUILD PRIOR KNOWLEDGE AT THE SENTENCE LEVEL

Having a lot of knowledge is foundational in successful reading. Willingham (2017) reported that a study conducted by Anne Cunningham and Keith Stanovich (1997) measured the reading ability of eleventh graders as well as their knowledge of mainstream culture. The researchers gave students "tests of the names of artists, entertainers, military leaders, musicians, philosophers, and scientists, as well as separate tests of factual knowledge of science, history and literature" (117). Their findings? There was a very strong correlation between the amount of cultural literacy that students possessed and their scores on reading tests. The more they knew, the better they read.

With this in mind, here are some ways to build students' prior knowledge that will help them understand at the sentence level.

Create a Sentence Study Unit

Students of all ages can benefit from a sentence study unit much like the one designed by Donna Santman, a remarkable middle school teacher (and now librarian) in New York City. Santman starts the unit by teaching some of the basics of the sentence: finding the subject and verb,[2] understanding dependent and independent clauses, and recognizing that not every noun is the subject of the sentence. Santman begins by sharing interesting sentences with her students and asking them: "What do you notice about these sentences? What decisions did the writer make in crafting them? What effect do these moves have on the reader?" She wants students to begin to see that the act of creating sentences is artistic, that there is intention behind their construction. She then encourages students to begin collecting sentences from their readings—sentences they find artful or that exhibit interesting decision-making by the writer.

2. Anyone who has taught high school for a while is dismayed—but not shocked—at the number of students who cannot identify the subject and verb in a sentence.

While students are in this collection mode, Santman selects sentences that lend themselves to imitation. In my classroom, for example, I used the first sentence of Matt de la Peña's *Mexican WhiteBoy*:

> **Dressed in a well-worn Billabong tee, camo cargo shorts and a pair of old-school, slip-on Vans, Danny Lopez follows his favorite cousin, Sofia, as she rolls up on the cul-de-sac crowd with OG swagger. (2018, 1)**

I then modeled how this sentence might be imitated:

> **Dressed in a hand-me-down, too-tight black suit and a pair of his father's oversize, scuffed wingtip shoes, Kelly Gallagher follows his older sister, Cathy, as they solemnly enter the dark church alongside other funeral mourners.**

Or I write another sentence that's inspired by the mentor sentence but deviates a bit more from its structure:

> **Trying to escape his parents, Jeremy Richards, wearing nothing but a pair of faded purple Rip Curl board shorts, shuffles through the sand with the weight of the world on his shoulders.**

Students then practice imitating a number of teacher-selected sentences over the next week or two. At the end of the unit, each student publishes their own sentences—sentences where they learned interesting ideas—by writing them on strips of paper and plastering them around the room.[3]

Santman also noticed an additional benefit that arose from this unit of sentence study. Before the unit, she noticed her students would often zoom in and pay attention only to the core of the sentences they were reading. They would often gloss over the nuances found in, say, a dependent clause that starts or ends a sentence, like in this example found in Jonathan Escoffery's *If I Survive You*:

> **On the day you are scheduled to begin the sixth grade, a hurricane named Andrew pops your house's roof open, peeling it back like the lid of a Campbell's soup can, pouring a fraction of the Atlantic**

3. I prefer using cash register tape for an activity like this. (Students can also use this tape for other purposes. For example, after reading *Hamlet*, each of my students found their favorite line, and my room became awash in the language of Shakespeare. Or have students find their favorite lines from the books they are reading independently.)

> **into your bedroom, living room—everywhere—bloating carpet, drywall, and fiberboard with sopping sea salt corrosion.** (2022, 12)

Students were likely to remember the core of the sentence (a hurricane badly damaged the house) but might forget that this tragic event happened to a sixth grader—a detail that adds another layer of meaning to the sentence.

Santman noticed that after studying numerous sentences over the course of this unit, her students became much more likely to attend to the entire sentence. They began to understand that a sentence's construction holds meaning. Gaining a deeper understanding of syntax made them better writers, but Santman also found that it made them better *readers*.

Try Sentence-Combining and Sentence-Revising Exercises

One of the most influential studies on the teaching of writing, *Writing Next* (Graham and Perin 2007), suggested eleven elements of effective adolescent writing instruction.[4] One of those key elements is teaching young writers to combine sentences.

I started by giving students two sentences:

> Sacramento is the capital of California.
>
> It is the fifth-largest city in the state.

I then modeled ways we could combine the two sentences:

> Sacramento, the fifth-largest city in the state, is the capital of California.
>
> Sacramento, the capital of California, is the fifth-largest city in the state.
>
> The capital of California, Sacramento, is the fifth-largest city in the state.
>
> The capital, Sacramento, is the fifth-largest city in California.
>
> The fifth-largest city in California—Sacramento—is the capital.

4. I would add one more: the building of prior knowledge. You have to know stuff to read stuff, but you *really* have to know stuff to write stuff.

Over a two-week period, I gave students two sentences daily to combine. Once they got the hang of that, we graduated to combining three sentences.

> I drove on the freeway.
>
> It was raining very hard.
>
> People were driving like maniacs.

Again, I modeled possibilities:

> Even though it was raining hard on the freeway, people drove like maniacs.
>
> People drove like maniacs on the freeway, despite the hard rain.
>
> Like maniacs, people drove through the hard rain on the freeway.
>
> On the freeway, people drove like maniacs through the hard rain.

Another way to build syntactic knowledge is through taking a simple sentence and having students play with revising it numerous times over several days. I modeled with the following sentence:

> The girl walked through the heavy snowfall.

Figure 3–4 contains several examples of possible revisions for this sentence.

We did this revision activity for a few minutes at a time over the course of a week and a half. On the first day, students started by writing simple sentences, and then each following day they began class by trying a new revision move (as modeled by the teacher).[5]

When students develop a deep background knowledge of sentence construction, they are more likely to comprehend challenging sentences.

Have Students Pick a Sentence of the Day

For this activity, after ten minutes of independent reading, each student revisits what they read and selects a sentence of the day. They can pick any sentence they find interesting—maybe they like its syntax or the writer's choice of diction, or perhaps

---

5. This focus on syntax presents an opportunity to have fun with sentences. It is a good place to introduce the dangling modifier (e.g., *Taped to the wall, Sal read the note*) so students can consider how sentence construction affects comprehension.

Revised Sentence	Move Made by the Writer
The girl trudged through the heavy snowfall.	Used a stronger verb
Melissa trudged through the heavy snowfall.	Named the subject
Exhausted, Melissa trudged through the heavy snowfall.	Added an adjective to start the sentence
Melissa, exhausted, trudged through the heavy snowfall.	Moved the adjective to the middle of the sentence
Melissa trudged through the heavy snowfall, exhausted.	Moved the adjective to the end of the sentence
Melissa, a senior in high school, trudged through the heavy snowfall.	Added an appositive
Trudging through the snowfall, Melissa, a senior in high school, headed home.	Rearranged to make it a complex sentence

Figure 3–4

they notice the writer has intentionally broken a rule for effect. Do this for two weeks and students will have collected ten interesting sentences in their notebooks. They can then choose their favorite sentence of the ten and write a brief reflection as to why it is their favorite. I distributed an index card to each student. The student wrote their favorite sentence on one side; they shared why it was their favorite on the other side. I then had students pass them and we did a read-around. At the end of this process, I had them emulate their favorite sentences.

Create Sentence Scrambles

Inspired by poetry refrigerator magnets, teacher Martin Brandt types up and divides sentences into grammatical chunks (2019, 39). For example, here is a sentence from the first paragraph of John Steinbeck's *Of Mice and Men*:

> On one side of the river the golden foothill slopes curve up to the strong and rocky Gabilan Mountains, but on the valley side the water is lined with trees—willows fresh and green with every spring, carrying in their lower leaf junctures the debris of the

winter's flooding; and sycamores with mottled, white, recumbent limbs and branches that arch over the pool. (2006, 1)

Here's how the sentence might be chunked out of order:

- carrying in their lower leaf junctures the debris of the winter's flooding
- and sycamores with mottled, white, recumbent limbs and branches that arch over the pool
- but on the valley side the water is lined with trees
- on one side of the river the golden foothill slopes curve up to the strong and rocky Gabilan Mountains
- willows fresh and green with every spring,

The teacher places each chunk on an individual index card and shuffles the deck. Students must then try to rearrange them into the original order. Once students have practiced this with a few sentences, they can create their own sentence scrambles.[6]

Study Punctuation

Another way to help students internalize the way sentences work is by giving them a passage with all the punctuation marks removed, like the one from Kristin Hannah's *The Four Winds* (2001) shown in Figure 3–5.

Kristin Hannah's Unpunctuated Passage	Kristin Hannah's Original Passage
Hope is a coin I carry an American penny given to me by a man I came to love there were times in my journey when it felt as if the penny and the hopes it represented were the only things that kept me going I came west in search of a better life but my American dream was turned into a nightmare by poverty and hardship and greed these past few years have been a time of things lost jobs home food. (1)	Hope is a coin I carry: An American penny, given to me by a man I came to love. There were times in my journey when it felt as if the penny and the hopes it represented were the only things that kept me going. I came west in search of a better life, but my American dream was turned into a nightmare by poverty and hardship and greed. These past few years have been a time of things lost: Jobs. Home. Food. (1)

Figure 3–5

6. For additional sentence instruction ideas, see Martin Brandt's *Between the Commas* (2019).

Put students in groups and ask them to punctuate the unpunctuated passage. Have each group share their guesses, and then reveal the original passage. This leads to interesting discussions about the decisions made by the writer (e.g., Why did Hannah use periods after *jobs*, *home*, and *food*? Why did she capitalize each word instead of simply having them as items in a series?). These conversations teach students that punctuation is artistic and should be carefully considered.

Model Sentence Crafting in Front of the Class

One way to help students develop syntactic maturity is to craft sentences in front of them (and to think out loud while doing so). I started with an easier example:

> **Tired from grading all those essays, the teacher walked out of the classroom and headed home.**

I asked the students if they liked this sentence or if they thought it was better if I rewrote it thus:

> **The teacher, tired from grading all those essays, walked out of the class and headed home.**

To help them make this decision, I placed the two sentences next to each other:

> **Tired from grading all those essays, the teacher walked out of the classroom and headed home.**
>
> **The teacher, tired from grading all those essays, walked out of the class and headed home.**

There was no right answer, I told them. But which one of them sounded better? Which one had better flow?

From there, I might show them two sentences that were a bit more complex:

> **My junior high school crush was Cyndi Bayless, who, although she sat next to me in Mrs. Carter's English class, had no idea I was alive.**
>
> **Cyndi Bayless, my junior high crush, who sat next to me in Mrs. Carter's English class, had no idea I was alive.**

It is important to not only ask them which one is better but to ask them *why* it is better. From there, encourage students to delve back into their writing notebooks and find a sentence they can rearrange. They should then ask their partner(s) which one is better—and why.

Play with Idioms, Adages, and Proverbs

Idioms are frequently used phrases or sentences that use figurative language to give a widely understood meaning.

Adages are sayings that have deeper meanings than the words read at face value and are considered by many to be true.

Proverbs often reflect commonsense advice.

Give students the list of thirty idioms, adages, and proverbs shown in Figure 3–6 and ask them how many they can decode.

Idioms	Adages	Proverbs
• jump on the bandwagon • bite the bullet • break a leg • burn the bridge • hit the sack • pull someone's leg • under the weather • break the ice • spill the beans • back against the wall	• Birds of a feather flock together. • Opposites attract. • Curiosity killed the cat. • The clothes make the man. • The early bird gets the worm. • Better late than never. • Two heads are better than one. • Fish and visitors stink after three days. • Love is blind. • There is no such thing as a free lunch.	• Strike while the iron is hot. • You can lead a horse to water, but you can't make it drink. • Don't judge a book by its cover. • An ounce of prevention is worth a pound of cure. • Don't cry over spilled milk. • If you lie down with dogs, you will wake up with fleas. • Too many cooks spoil the broth. • A bird in the hand is worth two in the bush. • An apple a day keeps the doctor away. • Nothing ventured, nothing gained.

Figure 3–6

Have them wrestle with these on their own for a few minutes, and then place students in small groups to try to fill in the gaps for those they do not know.[7] You could have each student choose their favorite one and connect it to a real-life experience in a quickwrite or a short paper.

THE IMPORTANCE OF PRIOR KNOWLEDGE AT THE PASSAGE LEVEL

Students often believe that comprehension is a yes-or-no proposition. Either you understand what you are reading, or you don't. But that is not how comprehension works. It is more nuanced than that. Consider this sentence:

> **My father came home to find me standing in front of a roaring fire.**

There is no difficult vocabulary here, but you can't fully comprehend the sentence without knowing what follows it. Notice how your comprehension shifts when you read the subsequent sentence:

> **My father came home to find me standing in front of a roaring fire. That made him mad, as we did not have a fireplace.**

You cannot understand sentence A without first possessing the knowledge found in sentence B. One sentence *builds* upon another. Comprehension *evolves* through the collection and connection of ideas. Sometimes I introduced this concept with a joke:

> **"I don't think I look thirty. Do you think I look thirty?" the husband asked.**
>
> **"No, dear," the wife replied, "but you used to."**

As a reader, our job is to hold on to bits of information as the passage unfolds. Your comprehension *progresses* as you read. As you acquire new knowledge, your

---

7. This activity benefits all students, but it is really helpful for those who are learning English as a second language.

Lines from the Prologue	How a Reader's Comprehension Evolves the Deeper She Gets into the Text
Two households, both alike in dignity, In fair Verona, where we lay our scene,	OK, this is a play that will involve two noble families who live in Verona.
From ancient grudge break to new mutiny, Where civil blood makes civil hands unclean.	Oh, wait. These families do not get along. There is a long, bloody history between them.
From forth the fatal loins of these two foes A pair of star-crossed lovers take their life;	What? It gets worse! Two ill-fated lovers from these bloodlines commit suicide.
Whose misadventured piteous overthrows Doth with their death bury their parents' strife.	At least something good comes from this—their deaths end the long-running feud.

Figure 3–7

understanding shifts and deepens. To illustrate this shift, let's look at the first eight lines of the prologue to *Romeo and Juliet*[8] (Shakespeare 2009, 1), shown in Figure 3–7.

I understand the first two lines, but I understand them more after I read the next two lines. And then I understand those four lines even more after I read the next two lines. And so on. I am building my comprehension bit by bit, which means I must learn to live with ambiguity as this construction occurs.

Studying how comprehension is layered in a paragraph also presents an opportunity to teach the concept of unity to young writers. Sometimes students write paragraphs that do not build properly—they tackle too many topics, or they jump all over the place.[9] To help students grasp this idea, I gave them a paragraph like this one and asked them which sentence did not belong:

> **A *quinceañera* is a celebration of a girl's 15th birthday. It has pre-Columbian roots in Mexico (Aztecs) and is widely celebrated by girls throughout Latin America. The Day of the Dead (Día de Muertos) is another popular holiday traditionally celebrated on November 1 and 2, primarily in Mexico. The girl celebrating her 15th birthday is a quinceañera (Spanish pronunciation: [kinsea'ɲeɾa];**

8. Spoiler alert!

9. We also want students to know that sometimes a paragraph is a single sentence. Or a single word.

> **feminine form of "15-year-old"). In Spanish, and in Hispanic America, the term quinceañera is reserved solely for the honoree; in English, primarily in the United States, the term is used to refer to the celebrations and honors surrounding the occasion.[10]**

The sentence that does not belong is the second one, as it deviates from the topic of the paragraph (a quinceañera). Exercises like this are helpful for students who try to jam too much into a single paragraph.

INTRODUCING PRIOR KNOWLEDGE AT THE PASSAGE LEVEL

When I had students read passages, I started by introducing a big idea: *Authors assume you know things.* No writer can begin from scratch, explaining every term, providing all the context needed. Writers assume you have background knowledge.

Let's look at this excerpt from Daniel James Brown's *The Boys in the Boat*. As you read it, consider what Brown assumes you know:

> **Increasingly there were distant and dark rumblings from Germany, intimations of the third and most tragic act. On October 14, Hitler had abruptly quit the League of Nations and discounted Germany's ongoing disarmament talks with France and her allies. It was a deeply disturbing turn of events, essentially abrogating the Treaty of Versailles and undermining the foundations on which European peace had been built since 1919. Krupp, Germany's legendary armament and munitions manufacturer, had begun secretly working on an initial order of 135 Panzer I tanks. Observers in Panama had recently noticed an enormous surge in the number of shipments of nitrates—used in the manufacturing of munitions—passing through the canal under blind sailing orders, en route from Chile to the Azores, heading in the direction of Europe, ultimate destination unknown. (2015, 76)**

10. Wikipedia (Wikimedia Foundation 2022) is the source for this paragraph. I added the sentence that does not belong. You can find many "Which sentence does not belong?" exercises online.

Brown assumes a lot here. He assumes you know geography: Panama, Chile, the Azores. He assumes you know history: the League of Nations, the Treaty of Versailles, the fact that 1919 immediately followed World War I, what a Panzer I tank is. He assumes you know words: *intimations*, *abrogating*. And he assumes that you know that the phrase *third act* refers to the final act of a story (or in this case, a war). Brown had to make these assumptions, because no writer can start from scratch and explain everything.

When my students have trouble reading a novel, it is often directly tied to the fact that what they are reading is far away from any prior knowledge they possess. Take the first four paragraphs of *To Kill a Mockingbird*, for example. Harper Lee assumes the reader knows the following: Andrew Jackson, the Creeks, the Battle of Hastings, Methodists, Cornwall, John Wesley's strictures, apothecaries, and chattels. My students in California always struggled with the beginning of this novel because Lee assumed they knew things that they did not know.

Writers invite us to take a role that may be familiar to their typical reading community but unfamiliar to others. Reading *Educational Leadership* or *Sports Illustrated* is not hard for me. These publications are written for me. This book you are holding is written for teachers, and because you are a teacher, it is not hard for you. I can reasonably assume you know some things about teaching. Otherwise, this book would be much longer.

☆—☆—☆

The quinceañera passage on page 70 is a good example of how comprehension evolves through the accumulation of prior knowledge, but sometimes a passage is so far removed from our backgrounds that it is hard to grasp much meaning. Take this passage, from a video game review, for example, which was written for gamers:

> ***Rivers of Blood*** **is a unique weapon which primarily scales with the Arcane stat and causes immense bleed damage. Its special skill, Corpse Piler,[11] has become a menace and a meme because it's so easy to use. Corpse Piler can be countered in PvP, but it's nearly peerless as a PvE boss-eater, dealing heavy damage and stagger from a safe distance while also triggering the bleed effect. Many players have long suspected that it would be nerfed one day, just as the powerful katana Moonveil was. (Wood 2022)**

11. Corpse Piler would be a great name for a metal band.

I am a strong reader, but when I read this passage, I realize I am also a weak reader. The author assumes that the reader has gaming experience and knows the difference between a PvE boss-eater and the powerful katana Moonveil. I simply do not possess enough requisite knowledge about gaming to make sense of this.[12] It is important that students see their teacher struggle to make sense of passages. It reinforces the idea that people never stop learning how to read—even English teachers—and that the more knowledge we acquire, the easier reading becomes.

HOW TO HELP READERS BUILD PRIOR KNOWLEDGE AT THE PASSAGE LEVEL

Whenever I considered how to help students become better readers, I started with a tough passage, like this one, written by Stephen Witt (2022) in the *New Yorker*:

> Imagine two pebbles thrown into a placid lake. As the stones hit the surface, they create concentric ripples, which collide to produce complicated patterns of interference. In the early twentieth century, physicists studying the behavior of electrons found similar patterns of wavelike interference in the subatomic world. This discovery led to a moment of crisis, since, under other conditions, those same electrons behaved more like individual points in space, called particles. Soon, in what many consider the most bizarre scientific result of all time, the physicists realized that whether an electron behaved more like a particle or more like a wave depended on whether or not someone was observing it. The field of quantum mechanics was born.

---

12. I knew I was in trouble when I read the title for this article: "Elden Ring Players Flabbergasted as the Infamous Rivers of Blood Katana Dodges Nerfs Yet Again."

If I were to have students read this passage, I would ask myself three key questions, which I suggest in *Deeper Reading* (2004, 198):

1. What do I want students to take from this passage?
2. How much will they understand without my help?
3. What can I do to bridge this gap?

See Figure 3–8 for a visual of these three questions.

To understand this, let's look at the vocabulary students would need in order to make sense of this passage (see Figure 3–9).

Figure 3–8

What vocabulary will students need to know to understand this passage?	What vocabulary will they understand without my help?	What terms will I need to teach to close this gap?
• concentric • electrons • subatomic • particles • waves • quantum mechanics	• electrons • waves	• concentric • subatomic • particles • quantum mechanics

Figure 3–9

What I did *before* they read the text was often more important than reading the text itself. I needed to frame the text before students read it. In this case, framing would mean front-loading vocabulary instruction.

Beyond framing the passage, here are some other ways to teach students the importance of prior knowledge when reading passages.

Pick a Passage

Have students select a passage from a book where they think prior knowledge is critical. Next they make a T-chart and place the passage on the left-hand side. On the right-hand side, they explain what prior knowledge a reader would need to make sense of it. Finally, they share in small groups or with the whole class.

Write a Passage

Have students write a passage for which they possess prior knowledge that others may lack. Model this first by writing one yourself. Again, I adopt a T-chart approach (see Figure 3–10).

Pick a TikTok Video

Much like the previous activity, ask students to select a TikTok video that requires prior knowledge to understand it. They can pick one that they think the teacher will have a hard time understanding, or they can select one they think may challenge their peers in small groups. Have them identify the knowledge needed to make sense of the video.

If we want our students to be critical readers of videos, we might also ask students to read a TikTok video critically. My Magnolia High School colleagues Taylor Thorne

My Written Passage	**Translation**
That little grom knows how to shred. He has been barreling all day. It helped that it was very glassy, for most of the day, but he bailed once it got blown out.	That little surfing prodigy is an expert surfer. He was getting tubed all day. It helped that the water was calm, but he left when the wind started to make the water too choppy.

Figure 3–10

and Angela Landre asked their students to find news-related videos on TikTok and answer the following via short video presentations:

- What or who is the news source? What do we know about this source?
- What is the central news of the video?
- What is not said in the video? What gaps of knowledge remain?
- Choose something the video leaves out and research this gap.
- What else should the viewer of this video know?

Their students submitted many interesting entries. Tyler, for example, shared a story about how some schools are using a controversial practice called seclusion rooms, where highly disruptive students are placed in holding cells. Tyler correctly noted that the news story left a lot out: How many schools do this? What are some of the specific reasons that students are isolated? Have these students endangered others? Are the teachers properly trained? How much are the parents involved? Tyler suggested that much of this information was intentionally left out "to cause drama and to get some clicks." Delilah, another student, found a news story that claimed that eating one egg a day causes more negative health effects than smoking five daily cigarettes. She noted, however, that nowhere in the piece was the actual study shared or cited, casting immediate doubt to its veracity. When asked what else the viewer of this video should know, Delilah shared that further research led her to see many of the benefits of eggs: they provide nutrients and protein, they help bone development, they boost one's immune system, and they help maintain metabolism and liver function.[13]

My colleagues followed up this assignment with another in which they asked students to find "informational" videos on TikTok that knowingly spread misinformation. These videos were not difficult to find, as one recent study found that almost 20 percent of TikTok videos contain

13. In *Outlive: The Science and Art of Longevity*, Dr. Peter Attia (2023) notes that the dire warnings about eggs as a source of harmful cholesterol have been overblown. We excrete almost all of the cholesterol we get from consuming food. "The vast majority of the cholesterol in our circulation is actually produced by our own cells" (118).

some misinformation (Brewster et al. 2022). This is alarming, as about one-third of adults under the age of thirty now regularly get their news on TikTok (Matsa 2023). Once students found misleading videos, they explained how they were able to tell that the video content was false. To help them complete this step, the teachers conducted minilessons on how to read videos critically. This included how to tell if a photograph is doctored or staged, how to recognize when a video clip may have been taken out of context, and how to discern whether audio is authentic or has been dubbed. (If you want to teach these skills, start with the video titled "3 Ways TikTok Content May Be Tricking You" [CBS Kids News 2023], which is readily available on YouTube.) Citing credible sources, students then corrected the misinformation.

Working together, Sheiden, Jasmin, and Shay conducted research that refuted many claims made by a video promoting a lectin-free diet. The information was presented by a certified life coach. The students began to realize that the information was likely suspect when they found out other websites had this same "certification"—and discovered those credentials were handed out for a nominal fee. They also challenged some of the dietary claims, providing research to debunk many of them. Throughout the class, students delved into many other videos, ranging from a deep-fake video of Barack Obama to a spokesperson making incorrect claims about autism, to false claims being made about sunscreens. This assignment enabled students to see how vulnerable one is when gathering "news" without prior knowledge.

I didn't have students do all of the previous activities at once. Rather, they did them over the course of the year to provide a periodic boost when reading motivation began to lag. Following is one more.

Read with Your Phone Next to You

When I read something confusing, I often grab my phone to google it, or I go to one of my favorite apps, Dictionary.com. Having instant access to information helps even the playing field when I lack essential prior knowledge.[14] I tell students that if they are reading something challenging, they need to turn off all notifications. A phone that constantly distracts you while you read challenging texts will make it *harder* to comprehend.[15]

---

14. One of the reasons I love my Kindle is that I can tap a word and instantly get its definition.

15. The strategy of keeping a phone nearby helps boost comprehension on all levels: word, passage, article, and book.

THE VALUE OF PRIOR KNOWLEDGE IN READING TEST PASSAGES

I have been in a lot of school districts where a heavy emphasis is placed on the reading of short passages. Why? Because this is the kind of reading valued on the state reading assessments.[16] Since these are the tests by which the effectiveness of teachers and schools is assessed, this kind of reading practice receives disproportionate attention in the curricula. (As Jim Cox, a former director of assessment in my school district, once said, "Always remember WYTIWYG." Pronounced "wittywig," this acronym stands for "What you test is what you get." If you test it, teachers will teach it.)

Given the importance that passage study plays in teacher evaluations, we should be mindful of two prior knowledge issues that deeply influence a reader's comprehension: the reader's level of word ownership and the level of background knowledge brought to the topic at hand.

Take, for example, a passage titled "Moving to the Back of Beyond" (2019), which is found in a Smarter Balanced practice test. The reader of this short passage is confronted with the following words: *penchant*, *unconventional*, *chaparral*, *vacillated*, *planetarium*, and *Coulter pine*. Students suffering from word poverty will have a tough time with this passage. Or consider a passage like "Blue Crabs Provide Evidence of Oil Tainting Gulf Food Web" (Associated Press 2019), found in another practice test. This passage explains how the Gulf Coast oil spill endangered sea life. This short passage assumes the reader knows the following terms: *larvae*, *metabolize*, *dispersant*, *spawning*, *repository*, *estuaries*, *sustenance*, and *shoals*. Certainly, a student who has studied marine biology is going to understand this passage at a deeper level than a student who is unfamiliar with the terms, even if they have the same reading ability.

When thinking about the importance that prior knowledge of words and concepts plays in reading a passage, consider "How Prior Knowledge Affects Word Identification and Comprehension," a study conducted by Priebe, Keenan, and Miller (2011), which found the following:

- "A child's skill at accurately reading a passage depends not just on their decoding skill but also on their knowledge of that passage topic; knowledge that also facilitates comprehension."

16. You can't assess the reading of a novel on a onetime on-demand test, as you cannot assume that every student in the state has read the same novel.

- Prior knowledge about the topic of a passage enables both greater comprehension of the text and better memory for it.
- Prior knowledge effects on comprehension are strongest for poor readers (citing Miller and Keenan [2009]). Poor readers with prior knowledge read passages more fluently, made fewer errors, and recalled significantly more ideas than poor readers without prior knowledge.
- "Struggling readers will be seen as having poor word decoding when in fact part of their struggles may also reflect low familiarity with the topic."

This study, and many others, raise questions: Is it fair to test all students of all backgrounds on a single, randomly selected passage? Do these scores accurately reflect each student's reading ability? Or are less privileged students (e.g., ones with a lack of access to books, fewer travel experiences) punished and often interpreted as having fixed inherited capacities? One recent study (Greene 2024) found these tests often measure prior knowledge more than anything.

CLOSING THOUGHTS

There is a movement away from long reading. Americans are reading fewer books, and the books they are reading are getting shorter (Gallup 2022). A study of 3,444 *New York Times* bestsellers between 2011 and 2021 found that the average length of books decreased by fifty-one pages. There was also a 30 percent drop in long books being published (Curcic 2022).

People are reading fewer books, but this does not mean they are reading less. It *does* mean their reading is shifting to shorter texts. With the prevalence of cell phones, the influence of social media, and the advent of click-and-go reading, it is imperative that students sharpen their short reading skills. This begins with teaching students—even high school students—how to closely read sentences, as understanding sentence structures is foundational to comprehension. Shanahan (2022) notes, "If all students did equally well on decoding, vocabulary, and memory tests, we'd still see variations in reading comprehension ability because of syntax difference. *The kids who understand syntax comprehend better than the ones who don't*" (italics mine). Understanding *what* a sentence says starts with having knowledge of *how* a sentence is constructed.[17]

17. Francis Christensen, a professor of English at the University of California, began advocating as early as the 1960s for teachers to spend more time teaching students to write at the sentence level. Christensen's "pedagogy consisted of short base-level sentences to which students were asked to attach increasingly sophisticated systems of initial and modifying clauses and phrases" (Connors 2000, 99). His theory was simple: If you can write good sentences, you can be a good writer.

Along with knowledge of words and syntax at the sentence level, readers also need general knowledge to assist in comprehending short passages like this one:

> **The bowler bowls from just beside the wicket at the other end of the pitch. At the same time, the other members of the bowler's team stand in various positions around the field acting as fielders. If the batsman misses the ball, and the ball hits the wickets, he is out and his turn to bat is over. If he hits the ball into the air and a fielder catches it, he is out. If a ball which the umpire thinks is going to hit the wicket is blocked by batsman's legs, he is out lbw (leg before wicket). But if the batsman hits the ball, he and his batting partner, who is standing at the other end of the pitch, can run to the opposite ends of the pitch to score one run. They can score two runs by each running back again. Three runs are scored if each batsman runs three lengths of the pitch, and so on. (Errey n.d.)**

I've read this passage three times, and I still do not fully comprehend it. Understanding every word and recognizing the syntactical moves were helpful but not enough. I simply do not have enough knowledge of the sport of cricket to thoroughly understand what I am reading. Being a good reader doesn't matter. Even at the sentence and passage levels, an experienced reader still needs to know stuff to read stuff.

WORKS CITED

Associated Press. 2019. "Blue Crabs Provide Evidence of Oil Tainting Gulf Food Web." In *Smarter Balanced Assessment Consortium: ELA Practice Test Scoring Guide, Grade 11*, 14–17. Los Angeles: Smarter Balanced Assessment Consortium. https://portal.smarterbalanced.org/library/en/grade-11-ela-practice-test-scoring-guide.pdf.

Attia, Peter. 2023. *Outlive: The Science and Art of Longevity.* With Bill Gifford. New York: Harmony.

Bagley, Pat. 2022. "Mike Lee Pledges to Serve Only Two Terms." Political cartoon. *Salt Lake Tribune*, November 9.

Brandt, Martin. 2019. *Between the Commas: Sentence Instruction That Builds Confident Writers (and Writing Teachers).* Portsmouth, NH: Heinemann.

Brewster, Jack, Lorenzo Arvanitis, Valerie Pavilonis, and Macrina Wang. 2022. "Beware the 'New Google': TikTok's Search Engine Pumps Toxic Misinformation to Its Young Users." NewsGuard. September 14. https://www.newsguardtech.com/misinformation-monitor/september-2022/.

Brown, Daniel James. 2015. *The Boys in the Boat: Nine Americans and Their Epic Quest for Gold at the 1936 Berlin Olympics.* New York: Penguin.

CBS Kids News. 2023. "3 Ways TikTok Content May Be Tricking You | CBS Kids News." CBS Kids News, May 30. YouTube video, 5:23. https://www.youtube.com/watch?v=w9xg09_eiP0.

Christensen, Francis. 1963. "A Generative Rhetoric of the Sentence." *College Composition and Communication* 14 (3): 155–61.

Connors, Robert J. 2000. "The Erasure of the Sentence." *College Composition and Communication* 52 (1): 96–128.

Cunningham, Anne E., and Keith E. Stanovich. 1997. "Early Reading Acquisition and Its Relation to Reading Experience and Ability 10 Years Later." *Developmental Psychology* 33 (6): 934–45. https://psycnet.apa.org/record/1997-43226-005.

Curcic, Dimitrije. 2022. "Bestselling Books Have Never Been Shorter." WordsRated. June 20. https://wordsrated.com/bestselling-books-have-never-been-shorter/.

Errey, Matt. n.d. "Cricket Vocabulary." EnglishClub. https://www.englishclub.com/vocabulary/sports-cricket.php.

Escoffery, Jonathan. 2022. *If I Survive You*. New York: MCD.

Gallagher, Kelly. 2004. *Deeper Reading: Comprehending Challenging Texts, 4–12*. Portsmouth, NH: Stenhouse.

Graff, Gerald, and Cathy Birkenstein. 2006. *They Say / I Say: The Moves That Matter in Academic Writing*. New York: W. W. Norton.

Graham, Steve, and Dolores Perin. 2007. *Writing Next: Effective Strategies to Improve Writing of Adolescents in Middle and High Schools*. Washington, DC: Alliance for Excellent Education. https://media.carnegie.org/filer_public/3c/f5/3cf58727-34f4-4140-a014-723a00ac56f7/ccny_report_2007_writing.pdf.

Greene, Peter. 2024. "Research Shows What State Standardized Tests Actually Measure." *Forbes*, February 10. https://www.forbes.com/sites/petergreene/2024/02/10/research-shows-what-state-standardized-tests-actually-measure/?sh=58bf60075e5d.

Jones, Jeffrey M. 2022. "Americans Reading Fewer Books than in Past." Gallup. January 10. https://news.gallup.com/poll/388541/americans-reading-fewer-books-past.aspx.

Lee, Harper. 2002. *To Kill a Mockingbird*. New York: HarperCollins.

Matsa, Katerina Eva. 2023. "More Americans Are Getting News on TikTok, Bucking the Trend Seen on Most Other Social Media Sites." Pew Research Center. November 15. https://www.pewresearch.org/short-reads/2023/11/15/more-americans-are-getting-news-on-tiktok-bucking-the-trend-seen-on-most-other-social-media-sites/.

Miller, Amanda C., and Janice M. Keenan. 2009. "How Word Decoding Skill Impacts Text Memory: The Centrality Deficit and How Domain Knowledge Can Compensate." *Annals of Dyslexia* 59 (2): 99–113.

Miller, Korin. 2023. "101 Chuck Norris Jokes to Make You Laugh." *Parade Magazine*, updated November 7. https://parade.com/968666/parade/chuck-norris-jokes/.

Misdea, Dan. 2023. "Daily Cartoon: Thursday, March 16th." *The New Yorker*, March 16. https://www.newyorker.com/cartoons/daily-cartoon/thursday-march-16th-march-madness.

"Moving to the Back of Beyond." 2019. In *Smarter Balanced Assessment Consortium: ELA Practice Test Scoring Guide, Grade 9*, 3–5. Los Angeles: Smarter Balanced Assessment Consortium. https://portal.smarterbalanced.org/library/en/grade-9-ela-practice-test-scoring-guide.pdf.

Peña, Matt de la. 2018. *Mexican WhiteBoy*. New York: Ember.

Priebe, Sarah J., Janice M. Keenan, and Amanda C. Miller. 2011. "How Prior Knowledge Affects Word Identification and Comprehension." *Reading and Writing* 7: 581–86. https://www.ncbi.nlm.nih.gov/pmc/articles/PMC3142886/.

Ramkumar, Amrith. 2022. "Bahamian Attorney General Defends Handling of FTX Collapse." *The Wall Street Journal*, November 27. https://www.wsj.com/articles/bahamian-attorney-general-defends-handling-of-ftx-collapse-11669597384.

Saunders, George. 2021. *A Swim in a Pond in the Rain: In Which Four Russians Give a Master Class on Writing, Reading, and Life*. New York: Random House.

Shakespeare, William. 2009. *Romeo and Juliet*. Mineola, NY: Dover Publications.

Shanahan, Timothy. 2022. "Trying Again—What Teachers Need to Know About Sentence Comprehension." *Shanahan on Literacy* (blog), August 13. https://www.shanahanonliteracy.com/blog/trying-again-what-teachers-need-to-know-about-sentence-comprehension.

Steinbeck, John. 2006. *Of Mice and Men*. New York: Penguin Books.

Wexler, Natalie. 2023. "Developing Knowledgeable Readers." ASCD. December 1. https://www.ascd.org/el/articles/developing-knowledgeable-readers.

Wikimedia Foundation. 2022. "Quinceañera." Wikipedia. November 18. https://en.wikipedia.org/wiki/Quinceanera.

Willingham, Daniel T. 2017. *The Reading Mind: A Cognitive Approach to Understanding How the Mind Reads*. San Francisco: Jossey-Bass.

Witt, Stephen. 2022. "The World-Changing Race to Develop the Quantum Computer." *The New Yorker*, December 12. https://www.newyorker.com/magazine/2022/12/19/the-world-changing-race-to-develop-the-quantum-computer.

Wood, Austin. 2022. "Elden Ring Players Flabbergasted as the Infamous Rivers of Blood Katana Dodges Nerfs Yet Again." GamesRadar+, April 19. https://www.gamesradar.com/elden-ring-players-flabbergasted-as-the-infamous-rivers-of-blood-katana-dodges-nerfs-yet-again/.

Knowing stuff positions students to challenge articles they are reading.
4

The Importance of Prior Knowledge AT THE ARTICLE LEVEL

Unlike reading a sentence or short passage, reading an article requires the reader to use prior knowledge to connect numerous ideas across paragraphs. This morning, for example, I read an article by Nobel Prize–winning economist Paul Krugman titled "Wonking Out: International Money Madness Strikes Again" (2023). Here are some of the concepts referred to in the op-ed:

hyperinflation

investment prospectuses

medium of exchange

store of value

unit of account

the Federal Reserve

debt ceiling

reserve-currency

Having prior knowledge of these terms is a prerequisite for understanding the article at a "What does it say?" level.[1] Krugman discusses hyperinflation early in the article. If you do not understand the concept of hyperinflation, you cannot follow his argument as he segues to the idea that hyperinflation may be putting the reserve-currency at risk. And if you don't understand what the reserve-currency is . . . well, you get the point. A leads to understanding B, B then leads to understanding C, and so on. The reader needs a lot of prior knowledge to make these connections throughout this twenty-paragraph article.

And that's just one article. If we want to build an informed citizenry, our students are going to need to know a lot of things. As I wrote this paragraph, I clicked on the front page of the *Wall Street Journal*. Here's the gist of the articles found only on the front page:

- Yellen Says US Economy Positioned for a Soft Landing
- Tesla Recalls Millions of Vehicles over Autopilot Concerns
- The Supreme Court Will Decide on Access to Abortion Pills
- The COP28 Climate Talks in Dubai Lead to Historic Deal to Phase Out Fossil Fuels
- Israel Begins Pumping Seawater into Hamas Tunnels in Gaza Strip
- Treasury Yield Slip Ahead of Fed Decision
- Scientists Closing in on a Cure for Morning Sickness
- Hunter Biden Defies GOP Subpoena

A reader of this issue of the *Wall Street Journal* would have to possess an impressive amount of prior knowledge to make sense of such a wide range of events. It seems paradoxical, but to help prepare students to read articles, we have to give them lots of articles (beyond the traditional curriculum) to read. And this should occur in all content areas.

---

1. Which brings to mind the value in preteaching academic language and some key concepts *before* students read challenging texts.

BUILD BACKGROUND KNOWLEDGE THROUGH THE ARTICLE OF THE WEEK

In *Readicide* (2009), I tell the story about the time I realized not a single ninth-grade student in two of my classes could name the vice president of the United States (It was Dick Cheney at the time). That was an epiphany for me—the moment when it registered that the school system was not producing young adults ready to actively engage in a participatory democracy.[2] They could identify the central theme in a novel, but they had no idea who their congressional representative was, or how many justices made up the Supreme Court, or what were the key propositions in the upcoming election.

Evidence of this lack of cultural literacy still abounds. The Annenberg Public Policy Center, in its annual Constitution Day survey (2022), found the following responses from adults:

- Forty-four percent were unable to name all three branches of government.
- Twenty-five percent could not name a single branch of government.
- Twenty-six percent could not name a single right guaranteed by the First Amendment.
- Forty-five percent did not understand what it meant when the Supreme Court ruled five to four in a case.

Only 4 percent of high school seniors score advanced in civic knowledge, "a level we would hope our future leaders would attain," said Charles N. Quigley, the executive director of the nonprofit Center for Civic Education (in Robelen 2011).

You may have also seen the YouTube video where several students on the campus of George Mason University were unable to identify photographs of Ronald Reagan and Joe Biden (at that point in time, Biden had been vice president for seven years)[3] (PoliTech 2016). They were, however, able to easily identify Kim Kardashian. PoliTech (2014) produced another video on the campus of Texas Tech University, where

---

2. Since 2009, the entertainment bubble students live in has only grown larger and more insular.

3. George Mason University is located nineteen miles from the White House.

numerous students were unable to answer the question "Who won the Civil War?" Any quick online search will find numerous person-on-the-street interviews where Americans can't name the two countries that border the United States or can't explain why we celebrate the Fourth of July (Wilson 2022). Sadly, these videos are not hard to find.

This recognition that students need to build their background knowledge was the impetus for starting the article of the week (AoW) with my students nearly twenty years ago.[4] I explain the rationale and introduction of the AoW in *Readicide* (2009), but it is clear from many of the questions I still receive that I need to share a bit more detail.

When introducing the concept of the AoW, I started with the *why*. Why would we be reading and discussing AoWs over the course of the school year? I began by giving students a political cartoon like the one on page 59. I was careful to select a cartoon where they would know all the words but would have trouble comprehending because they lacked prior knowledge. I asked them why they did not understand the cartoon. Through class discussion, we established the idea that you have to know stuff to read stuff. Once they understood this notion, I shared a couple more examples (like the *Wall Street Journal* news articles referred to earlier in this chapter) until I was reasonably sure they grasped the importance of prior knowledge. I was honest with them: "There may be times when you will not like doing the AoWs. Remember: I do not select them to entertain you. I select them to *inform* you.[5] And sometimes there may be a topic that doesn't immediately grab your interest. Or you might not be in the mood to write your weekly reflection. But I promise you this: if you read and write responses to the AoWs, you will build a knowledge base that will make you a better reader and a better thinker *for the rest of your lives*. This is important, but it doesn't come easy. It requires hard and sustained work."

4. The AoWs on my website (https://www.kellygallagher.org) average nearly twelve thousand visits each week, giving hope that knowledge building is going on.

5. An article on the nation's debt ceiling crisis is not something they will find thrilling. But sometimes the AoW both entertains and informs (e.g., "Do Cell Phones Cause Cancer?").

I distributed the AoW every Monday and collected their responses every Friday. For each week's article, I asked students to first mark their confusion. I didn't want them hiding their confusion; I wanted them to *reveal* it. Confusion is normal, the place where learning occurs, and marking it has three benefits: (1) it helps students monitor *exactly* where their comprehension falters; (2) it encourages them to reread closely—rereading being the principal strategy strong readers employ when faced with confusion; and (3) it gives them a starting place to share their confusion with others in an attempt to wrestle with it. We didn't run from confusion; we embraced it.

When students get an article that is hard for them to understand, they are forced to be metacognitive (this is a good thing). We should teach them to ask themselves two questions when confronted with confusion: Where, exactly, does my comprehension break down? What do I already know that may be helpful in understanding the hard parts? I want students to understand that because of their limited knowledge, they are going to run into a lot of things they do not fully grasp. When this happens, I do not want them to internalize this as a shameful thing ("I am stupid" or "I'm helpless"). This is not a failure on their behalf; instead, it just means they have to consciously work on strengthening their background knowledge. Ignorance is the problem, not intelligence.

The second thing I asked them to do was show evidence of thinking on the page. They could challenge ideas, ask questions, make predictions, form an interpretation, make connections, seek clarifications, make inferences—anything that showed they were thoughtfully interacting with the article. I wanted to see what they were thinking *as they were reading the text.* Much of this thinking cannot be done if students do not read closely. In fact, one clear sign of a shallow reading is when the reflection is about the headline topic, not about the specifics found inside the article.

The last requirement was to write a one-page reflection (not a summary) by hand, which they then attached to the article before turning it in. Students responded in any way they found meaningful, and for those who had trouble generating ideas, I offered the following possible questions:

- What are your thoughts about ______________? Explain.
- Did something in the article surprise you? Discuss.
- Pick a word, line, or passage from the article and respond to it.
- Is there something in this article that you'd like to talk back to?
- Discuss a move made by the writer in this piece that you think is good or interesting.[6] Explain.

---

6. A move is anything the writer did that made the writing interesting or helped the reader understand the article (e.g., the use of metaphor or decisions regarding word choice or syntax).

These prompts were intentionally open ended, and students were free (and encouraged) to ignore them if they had different reflections in mind. I wanted students to generate their own thinking. If I asked them narrower questions, then I'd be determining exactly what they would think (and what they would not think). I tried to avoid that. I wanted my students to embrace the blank page. This is not easy to do at the beginning of the year, as many students would rather the teacher just hand them some questions. Reading as a simple extraction exercise is a lot easier than sharing what you think, and asking students to fill a page with their thinking breaks them of the habit of relying on the teacher to determine what they should think.

Like anything else I wanted students to do, I modeled how to do it. For the first AoW of the year, I interacted with it by writing and thinking out loud in front of the class. I responded to the same article differently each period to begin showing students a range of interactions. For example, in one class I responded to a key line, while in another class I made a connection between the article and a book I'd read. Once I collected the first batch of student work, I pulled exemplars and shared them, showing students a multitude of ways readers can respond meaningfully to text. I continued this level of modeling for the first three weeks of the school year and then began to gradually pull back once students started getting the hang of it. If, later in the year, the quality of the work began to lag—which often happened—then I returned to showing them more exemplary student work as a way of reminding them of the expectations. I also reminded them, again, *why* we were doing these.

The good news about this activity is that students mark many articles, and they write many reflections. The bad news is that the students mark many articles, and they write many reflections. This creates an enormous weekly paper load for the teacher. So how did I handle this? Each AoW was worth twenty points—ten points for interacting with the text and ten points for the weekly reflection. But here is my secret: I spent very little time grading them.[7] I looked at each paper for no more than ten seconds, taking a quick glance at the level of interaction and maybe reading a line or two in each reflection. That's it. No more than ten seconds per paper. "This one looks like an 18. This one is a 14. This one is a 20." Bam. Bam. Bam. I graded an entire class set in under five minutes. (Yes, I timed it).

I have seen the AoW adopted a number of different ways in a number of different places. That's what teachers do—take someone else's idea and adapt it to their students (I have done this countless times). My colleague Taylor Thorne has her students

7. Let's be honest. All grading is subjective. I graded them only because I had to. Grading did not make my students smarter. Reading and responding to the articles made them smarter. Attaching points to the work was a motivator for some students and appeased some parents. It demotivated other kids. Students also knew that they could redo any assignment that received a low grade. No grade was ever final unless the student decided so. And that was true for all assignments in my class, not just for AoWs.

select an article from *Upfront Magazine*, a Scholastic and *New York Times* publication that delves into current events.[8] Each student selects an article of interest and completes a T-chart with the headings "What Does It Say?" and "What Does It Not Say?" The student then creates a short video in which they

- introduce the article, author, and source
- explain the key points of the article
- comment on the gaps of information (What was not said?)
- introduce an area of focus (a gap they researched)
- present their findings
- conclude with an important takeaway

Myriam, a tenth grader, read "A New Kind of Smoking Ban," which detailed how New Zealand would be implementing a smoking ban for those born after 2008 (Grise and De Stefani 2023). Following the assignment guidelines, Myriam made a seventy-eight-second video; here's the transcript:

> I read the article "A New Kind of Smoking Ban." The article discussed how New Zealand is slowly working toward a smoke-free country. The article said, and I quote, "The national smoking rate for adults has halved in the past decade." But it didn't say how much it used to be. I think this would be important information because it would show how much progress the country has made. The article also said, "People are worried that this new ban will fuel a black market." But it didn't say how often or how usual it is for New Zealand to have a black market in the first place. New Zealand is kind of a small country, and not a lot of people know a lot of information about it, so I think some more background knowledge would have been more useful. It also says that "anyone born after 2008 will never be allowed to legally buy cigarettes." But it didn't mention other forms of smoking. So I did some digging and found out that vaping is still legal in New Zealand. So I wonder: how

8. I highly recommend this magazine as a means of building prior knowledge. At my school, we found funding to buy a weekly class set, and then we rotated that set among different teachers.

> **effective is banning smoking if people can just move to vaping? From this story, I think people should take away that humans tend to find loopholes in the rules. Thank you. Bye.**

Myriam's filmed reflection—and those of her classmates—were posted on the classroom digital page so that anyone in the class could view them.

I have also seen other teachers turn the AoW into elaborate assignments lasting an entire week or longer, but, for me, the AoW remained very simple: once the rhythm of the weekly assignment was established and students understood the expectations, I spent very little classroom time on it. I framed the article for a couple of minutes when I passed it out on Monday, and I collected it on Friday. That's it. Three to four minutes of class time a week. Because of this brevity, the AoW didn't replace any curriculum. It sat on top of the regular curriculum.

Some schools use the AoW in content areas other than English (e.g., "The Gaza Strip and Its History, Explained" in a government class or "The 'Forever Chemicals' in Our Water" in a science class). Some teachers in other content areas generate their own version of the AoW as well. One of my favorites is the graph of the week, which my friend and former colleague Kelly Turner uses in math classes. Her students not only learn math skills but also gain knowledge as they read and write about current events. Turner is more than a math teacher; she is a literacy builder. And the graphs she selects hold value in subjects beyond mathematics. (For more, see her website: https://www.turnersgraphoftheweek.com.)

CONSIDER THIS

Once every quarter I had students select their own articles. This had the added benefit of spurring them to research what was going on in the world and make decisions as to what was worth reading. When assigning this, I reminded them that the goal was to inform their fellow students about things they may not know about. Students shared their articles with their peers through a jigsaw activity. One caveat: many of my students did not have printers (or ink) at home, so I let them email their articles to me at school, and they came in before school to print them in my room.

HAVING PRIOR KNOWLEDGE ENABLES YOU TO TALK BACK

Prior knowledge is required to read at a literal level, but it is also foundational to reading *beyond* a literal level. Knowing things is also a critical component in having the ability to *talk back* to an article. We don't want students to simply understand what they are reading; we want them to be able to *challenge* what they are reading. And you can't challenge what you read (or hear) if you don't possess prior knowledge about the topic at hand.

A case in point: I recently read an article from the *New York Times* titled "Baseball Is Dying. The Government Should Take It Over" (Walther 2022). In this opinion piece, the author, Matthew Walther, argues that baseball appeals only to older people and the sport is in trouble because young people find baseball to be boring and slow.[9] Baseball's fan base is dwindling. To save the sport, Walther argues, the government should nationalize it and put it under the authority of a federal entity. Failure to do so, he asserts, will lead to the sport's extinction.[10]

What is more interesting to me is what the author *doesn't* say in his argument. He doesn't say that there is a greater chance that Bigfoot exists than there is of Congress seizing Major League Baseball. Any politician who would propose this would be crucified. Add a Supreme Court that leans strongly to the right (e.g., adverse to government intrusion in business affairs) and mix in antitrust laws, and this proposed solution is dead in the water. My ability to reject his argument is grounded in my knowledge of how Congress works, of the political underpinnings of the Supreme Court, and of antitrust laws. Knowing these things positions me to talk back to the piece.

Still, it is one thing to use prior knowledge to reject an idea; it's another thing to use it to propose an alternative course of action. So here is my response to the baseball article (grounded in my prior knowledge): If you want to ratchet up interest in baseball, start by addressing the competitive imbalance created by the revenue disparity that exists between teams. Some fans of small-market teams lose interest because they know their teams cannot compete with those teams with deep pockets. Shohei Ohtani, for example, signed a ten-year, seven-hundred-million-dollar contract with the Dodgers. There is no way that the Oakland Athletics can afford that, which is one reason why they ended up with the worst record in baseball in the 2023 season. Realistically, there is a group of small-market teams that have very little chance to regularly compete for a championship, and, as a result, their fans tune out. The NBA, the NFL, and the NHL all have salary caps that ensure that teams do not massively outspend one another; it is time for a salary cap to be implemented in baseball.

Knowing things gives me the ammunition to not only talk back to the argument but also think *beyond* the argument. And isn't that what we want for our students? To develop the ability to go deeper with the things they read and hear? To acquire as much

---

9. My favorite line: "Mike Trout's $426 million contract is effectively being paid by millions of grandparents who just want to tune in to Anderson Cooper or *Antiques Roadshow*." He also equates watching baseball with collecting 78 rpm records. Ouch.

10. Baseball is not dying. In the 2023 season—after this article was published—MLB had its highest attendance in thirty years. New rules shortened the games, making them more attractive.

knowledge as possible so as to position themselves to counter lawmakers, school board members, advertisers, bosses, bloggers, teachers, and others (like spouses)?

Jeff Wilhelm, noted teacher and author, reminds us that it is normal practice to do a significant amount of research before making a major purchase.[11] You wouldn't just rush out and buy a car without investigating its features and how this make and model stood up next to similar vehicles by other manufacturers. There are many angles to consider before deciding which car to buy. Yes, the car may get great gas mileage, but what is its safety crash rating? How much does it cost to insure? And what is its resale value? Wilhelm suggests we teach students this concept before they rush out and "buy" an idea or ideology. When you read someone's opinion—in an article, for example—you should carefully consider what is not said. What is being intentionally left out? What are the thoughts of the people who oppose this stance? It is hard, if not impossible, to do this if you lack necessary prior knowledge.

PRIOR KNOWLEDGE IN THE AGE OF CLICK-AND-GO READING

Until very recently, humans have never encountered digital click-and-go reading. This new type of reading is actually rewiring the brain in ways never seen before (Wolf 2019). For the first time, humans are bombarded with waves and waves of information. Go to any news website, left or right, and you will find numerous articles screaming for your attention. There is not enough time to read everything that is flying at us, so we are in a constant decision-making mode: *Which articles should I read? Which ones should I ignore?* And once you begin reading, there are *more* decisions to make. *Which hyperlinks am I going to click? Which will I skim past? How far down that rabbit hole am I willing to go?*

Much of this decision-making is grounded in our prior knowledge. Sitting at my computer this morning, I came across an article titled "IRS Plans to Hire Gun-Carrying Special Agents in All 50 States" (Revell 2023). I took a hard pass on reading it for a couple of reasons: I already knew that the IRS is arming some agents because arresting people who have criminally avoided paying taxes has become quite dangerous. I also checked where the article was published, noting that it came from a source with

11. I heard Jeff say this when I was a guest of the Boise State Writing Project, which he has led for twenty-one years.

a history of trying to scare its older-skewing audience—a source I rarely find newsworthy.

Nope, time to move on.

Another clue that helps me determine whether I will continue reading? I check to see if I recognize the author. I will read any movie review from Justin Chang, for example, but I try to avoid those written by Kenneth Turan. I have read Chang long enough to know that if he likes the movie, there is a very high probability that I will as well. I have disagreed with Turan so often that I stopped reading his reviews.

The danger here, of course, is that we rely on our prior knowledge in a way that leads us to read only people we like. Our brains are being manipulated and even rewired by algorithms that are designed to get our attention (Girish 2020).[12] AI (artificial intelligence) feeds us articles we want to read and shields us from other points of view. There is a danger to remaining in an echo chamber, as evident by the sharp and widening divide found in this country (and others). If we are to overcome this—if we stand any chance of breaking down these silos—we need to ensure that we hear a range of opinions. I encourage my friends on the left to regularly read conservatives they often disagree with—David Frum, Ana Navarro-Cárdenas, David Brooks, Joe Scarborough, Rich Lowry, and Joe Walsh.[13] And I likewise encourage my friends on the right to regularly read opposing views from Sherrilyn Ifill, David Rothkopf, Josh Marshall, Sarah Kendzior, Elizabeth Bruenig, and Mo Elleithee. It is unhealthy to ignore the "other side."

How did I come up with these lists of commentators? Again, prior knowledge. Through a history of reading and sorting through the noise, I have weeded out extremists, shucksters, and masters of spreading Bandini.[14] And, yes, this is an ongoing, never-ending, imperfect process, as my knowledge grows and shifts. But the more I read, the more I am able to determine if what I am reading is worth my attention.

As with the IRS article, sometimes prior knowledge can help you decide to *not* read an article. For another example, I recently stumbled across an article that claimed that Chelsea Clinton advocated for forcing every child in America to be vaccinated. Immediately, I wondered if that could possibly be true, so I looked to see what the source of the article was. It came from WND—an organization I had never heard of.

---

12. For more on the dangers of these algorithms, I recommend viewing Jeff Orlowsky-Yang's chilling documentary *The Social Dilemma*.

13. The Republican from Illinois, not the Eagles' guitarist.

14. Bandini is a type of fertilizer. Literal bullsh*t.

A couple more clicks revealed that this organization is known for promoting falsehoods and conspiracy theories, including the false claim that former president Barack Obama was not born in the United States. The Southern Poverty Law Center notes the WND's pages "are devoted to manipulative fear-mongering and outright fabrications designed to further the paranoid, gay-hating, conspiratorial and apocalyptic visions of [website founder Joseph] Farah[15] and his hand-picked contributors from the fringes of the far-right and fundamentalist worlds" (n.d.). A couple more clicks led me to Snopes, a fact-checking nonpartisan website, which confirmed that, indeed, the claim about Chelsea Clinton was false.

Readers can tell a lot from headlines. I am writing this on the day that a jury in New York found Donald Trump liable for sexual abuse and defamation in the E. Jean Carroll case. Here are three headlines from different publications—one from a far-left source, one from a moderate source, and one from a far-right source.[16] I have mixed up their order. Can you guess which is which?

1. Trump to appeal verdict in E. Jean Carroll civil case, says he has 'absolutely no idea' who she is
2. E. Jean Caroll's lawyers leveled a knockout blow to Trump
3. Trump found liable for defamation, sexual abuse in civil case

How did you do? Here is the answer key:

1. The source of this headline is Brooke Singman (2023), published on the Fox News website, which, according to AllSides, is a far-right news source. Note that the focus of the headline is on Trump's reaction rather than the jury's decision. (The headline also had a header above it that read, "Verdict is a disgrace." This despite it being a unanimous decision.)
2. The source of this headline is Mitchell Epner (2023), writing for the Daily Beast, which, according to AllSides, is a far-left news source. There is no evidence that this verdict is a knockout blow to Trump and his candidacy. In fact, a number of Republican senators rushed to his defense, calling the verdict a sham. Months later, Trump became the 2024 Republican candidate for president.

15. Joseph Francis Farah, the founder of the site.

16. These labels were determined by a multipartisan scientific analysis across online media sites. For more, go here: https://www.allsides.com/media-bias/media-bias-chart#methodology.

3. The source of this headline is James Fanelli and Corinne Ramey (2023) in the *Wall Street Journal*, which, according to AllSides, is a centrist news site.[17] Note that this headline simply reports what happened without infusing any editorializing.

Understanding the bias of news organizations has saved me from reading articles written to deceive or to falsely enrage. Prior knowledge provides a shield against click-bait and angertainment.

PRIOR KNOWLEDGE AND GENRE STUDY

People who read a lot of articles begin to develop an intuitive knowledge of what different kinds of articles will look and feel like. An op-ed article has a different look and feel than an obituary. An article in *Better Homes and Gardens* is going to look and feel different than an article in *Scientific American*. Each has its key functions, unique to its own purpose. People who read a lot of articles develop an intuitive knowledge of what to expect in a given text.

In *4 Essential Studies*, Penny Kittle and I (2021) discuss the value of teaching students to study essays from above, a perspective we call the drone view. We want students to stand above the piece as a whole, specifically analyzing the building blocks of its construction. ("This chunk of the article does this. The next chunk does that.") To illustrate this, let's look at the structure of a movie review—in this case, critic Brian Tallerico's review of the film *John Wick: Chapter 4*. Here are the drone-view chunks of his review:

Chunk 1: He recommends the film.

Chunk 2: He provides a summary of the film.

Chunk 3: He analyzes an element of the film (the choreography).

Chunk 4: He discusses the cast.

Chunk 5: He points out a flaw in the film.

Chunk 6: He returns to his recommendation to see it.

---

17. This is not to be confused with the *Wall Street Journal*'s op-ed page, which leans to the right.

Let's compare Tallerico's structure with a review of the same movie by critic Owen Gleiberman:

Chunk 1: He starts with a summary.

Chunk 2: He discusses the cast.

Chunk 3: He analyzes an element of the film (one character).

Chunk 4: He discusses a flaw in the film.

Chunk 5: He recommends the film.

Though the structure of the two reviews are different, they both contain elements one would expect to find in any movie review: a recommendation (or not), some summary, some analysis, a discussion of the film's flaws, and some information about the cast. When you read a lot of movie reviews, your prior knowledge of how that genre is constructed helps you read the articles at a deeper level.

Of course, we want to apply this thinking to other types of writing as well. Take op-eds, for example. As I was writing this chapter, my editor, Tom Newkirk, shared one he had written, "The Manufactured Reading Crisis."[18] Figure 4–1 shows how his essay is chunked.

When readers recognize the bones of an op-ed, they become more adept at understanding how this genre is constructed. I know, for example, that most op-eds include the following: a central argument, reasons and support for the argument, and a recognition and refutation of the other side. Often they will also weave in a narrative to support the argument.

Once my students understood how an op-ed is put together, I asked them to consider a possible different sequence. In Tom Newkirk's essay, for example, the thesis is stated in the conclusion. Would it have been better if it were placed in the introductory paragraph? Could the author have started with his reasons and support before transitioning to the prevailing view? Perhaps he should have started with the "why this is important and why the reader should care" segment. Ask your students: "Is this sequence better? Or is that sequence better? Which sequence has the best effect on the reader?" Students who internalize the drone view begin making organizational decisions when they write their own longer pieces.[19]

---

18. Read the op-ed here: https://www.atholdailynews.com/My-Turn-The-Manufactured-Reading-Crisis-52985661.

19. I learned this years ago when I was asked to write my first grant proposal. I struggled—until I found examples of other proposals. After I had read a few of them, they became much easier to understand, and internalizing their features helped me write my own.

Do We Have a National Reading Crisis?
Thomas Newkirk

Sets up the prevailing view

Well, that's the story.

A national reading crisis is a central part of now-familiar Science of Reading narrative. In short, our public schools have failed to adhere to scientific findings about reading acquisition—most notably the importance of phonics instruction—leading to children failing to establish the foundational skills for reading.

The key evidence for this crisis comes from the 2022 National Assessment for Educational Progress (NAEP) which found that only 33% of 4th grade students tested Proficient or Advanced. The overall performance in 2022 was equivalent to 1992 with the small gains over that period disappearing. This result led to alarming (but misleading) headlines about the majority of students struggling to read—a real crisis.

Pivots to his counterargument

But we need to pause, take a deep breath, and reflect on these results. To be sure, the lack of improvement is disappointing to educators who have put so much emphasis on supporting struggling readers. There is clearly work to be done—and no reason to be complacent.

Provides reasons and support for his argument

We could also conclude, more positively, that students taking the test in 2022 are reading as well as their parents when they were in school. In fact, the results of this and other tests, like the widely-respected PISA (Programme for International Student Assessment) tests, show essentially a flat line.

The cut-off points for any assessments are, to a considerable degree, arbitrary. Those for NAEP are particularly stringent, virtually guaranteed to assign the majority of students to below proficient. The levels produce what David Reinking, Georgy Hruby, and Victoria Risko have called a "ready-made crisis"

To make sense of these results, we need to place them in an international context. If U.S. students are broadly failing because of flawed teaching methods, we would expect to find them well behind students in other economically advanced countries. But that is not the case.

In the PISA 2018 assessment of high school reading, the United States placed ninth among the 38 economically advanced countries, about level with Sweden, the United Kingdom, Japan, and Australia-- and well above the international average.

We get similar results if we turn to the international performance of younger students. In the 2016 PIRLS (Progress in International Reading Study) the US was ranked 15 out of 50 countries, behind Finland, Sweden, and Hungry, but ahead of Denmark, the Netherlands, and Australia. The PIRLS ranking in 2021 was even higher, though we should be cautious about comparisons because of the pandemic.

Again, there is no evidence, in these respected studies, of a national reading crisis—though the assessments confirm troubling socio-economic gaps in the United States. In fact, the reading "penalty" for being poor in the United States is greater than in most of the countries tested. A U.S. student in the lowest quartile economically is far less likely to break into the top reading levels than similar students in other advanced countries. And this gap has widened during the pandemic.

Figure 4–1

(*continues*)

So why does all this matter?

A crisis mentality leads to abrupt, disruptive, top-down changes that force teachers to abandon approaches that have worked for their students. The pendulum swings. While advocates of the Science of Reading stress that phonics instruction is only one of many validated practices, the blunt message to schools is that it is the game-changer, the silver bullet—phonics programs are proliferating with large blocks of whole-class instruction devoted them, often for years.

Yet the research itself suggests that phonics instruction has only a moderate effect size and the evidence is weak that there is a significant benefit after K-1. But it can have a negative effect if it crowds out other powerful tools like teaching comprehension strategies and building vocabulary and prior knowledge. Or writing. Or simply the chance to read books. That's the conclusion of the oft-cited National Reading Panel report, published in 2000, which warned: "Phonics should not become the dominant component in a reading program, neither in the amount of time devoted to it nor in the significance attached."

addresses why this is important and why the reader should care

H. L. Mencken reportedly commented that "for every problem there is a solution that is simple, neat—and wrong." We naturally prefer a story in which right and wrong, good and bad, are neatly confronting each other. We long for the single cause. But not all children learn the same way, and children have learned to read in diverse countries, diverse eras, with diverse approaches. Science can identify trends and "effect sizes," but it cannot dictate the right action in any situation. That takes teacher judgment. It can't be legislated.

It's messy that way—and human.

ends the essay with his thesis statement

Figure 4–1 *Continued*

Having prior knowledge of the content is one thing; having prior knowledge of how genres are constructed is another. Having prior knowledge of both makes students better readers and writers.

INTRODUCING PRIOR KNOWLEDGE AT THE ARTICLE LEVEL

Here are some activities I have done with students to help them see the importance that prior knowledge plays when reading articles.

Understand the Gap

Students visit online news sites with the purpose of selecting two articles that interest them—one they understand and one they do not completely understand. Students write reflections as to why they understand the first article but not the other. Having them reflect on the gap between the two articles reinforces the idea that you have to know stuff to read stuff.

Shift Your Comprehension

Students find an article they do not thoroughly understand and score their level of comprehension on a 1–10 scale (1 is very poor comprehension; 10 is very strong comprehension). After scoring, they highlight any part of the article where their comprehension falters. Once they have identified these trouble spots, they have online access for fifteen minutes to research what they do not know. At the end of this research period, have them rescore their level of comprehension. Almost every student will score themselves higher. This presents an opportunity to ask them why their scores jumped. I always pointed out that their reading abilities did not change in the last fifteen minutes. What changed was that they built the necessary knowledge base so that when they reread, their comprehension improved.

Wrestle Collaboratively

Give students an article that will challenge them. After they have individually highlighted their trouble spots, place them in small groups and ask them if they can clear up their confusion. When finished, ask them three questions: (1) Who brought helpful prior knowledge to the discussion? (2) What prior knowledge proved most helpful? (3) What do you still need to know to improve your comprehension?

HOW TO HELP READERS UNDERSTAND THE IMPORTANCE OF PRIOR KNOWLEDGE AT THE ARTICLE LEVEL

Once students see the importance that prior knowledge plays at the article level, here are additional lessons to help them to cement their understanding.

Teach Students That Comprehension Is Fluid

I just finished watching the latest season of the television series *Fargo*. The series constantly flashes back and jumps into the future. Many episodes open with a scene that is confusing because it is shown without context—the viewer doesn't have enough of the story to figure out what is happening. Slowly, episode by episode, we patiently collect pieces of the puzzle, until, eventually, the big picture makes sense. But it wasn't easy getting there. I had to live in an extended state of ambiguity.

I wanted my students to understand that this is what proficient readers do. We read locally before we understand globally. To help them grasp this idea, I began by telling them a joke:

> A guy goes into a pet shop and tells the owner that he needs a pet for his mother. The guy says that his mom lives alone and could really use some company.
>
> The pet shop owner says, "I have just what she needs. A parrot that can speak in five languages. She'll have a lot of fun with that bird."
>
> The guy says he'll take the parrot and makes arrangements to have the bird delivered to his mom.
>
> A few days later, he calls his mother. "Well, Mom, how do you like that bird I sent?"
>
> She says, "Oh, son, he was delicious!"
>
> Aghast, the son says, "Mom, you ate that bird? Why, he could speak five languages!"
>
> The mom says, "Well, he should have said something!"

They didn't understand the joke until they heard the last line. That's when the global understanding emerged. To illustrate the importance of holding on to ambiguity as the joke unfolded, I didn't reveal the entire joke at once. Instead, I read one paragraph, stopped, and asked, "What do you think happens next?" I repeated this after each subsequent paragraph. At first, the predictions were all over the place, but as they got deeper into the joke, students started gaining a deeper understanding of where the joke might be going. Asking for predictions encourages students to revisit the text and teaches them how to start piecing things together. Most importantly, it teaches readers that comprehension unfolds and that proficient readers develop patience when they do not immediately understand everything.

We have all had this happen when reading: You are cruising along, thinking, *I am understanding this perfectly well*, when suddenly you hit a rough patch where you think, *Wait. Maybe I am not understanding this as well as I thought I did.* You stop and ask, *Huh? What is happening?* You backtrack and reread because you have become aware that you are unaware. Or the opposite occurs. You are struggling, concerned that you do not understand what you are reading, when suddenly it clicks and you realize, *Oh! I get it now!* When my students read *Dr. Jekyll and Mr. Hyde*, for example, they were mired in confusion for several chapters until that moment when the big reveal occurred. At that moment, everything snapped into place and their prior confusion began to make sense.

As stated earlier in the chapter, comprehension is not a yes-or-no proposition. It is ongoing and it shifts as we read. Students need to know this. Ask them, "Can you think of a movie where you were confused for a while, but you hung in there, and by the end of the movie you understood it?" The ability to hang in there when it was confusing is a skill, and this is the same skill we want them to develop as readers.[20]

Have Students Try to Stump the Teacher

Have students bring in an artifact (lyric, meme, tweet, cartoon) they believe will be puzzling to you. In front of the class, look at the items one at a time and try to explain what they mean. Students then explain what prior knowledge is necessary to understand each of them.

Frame Difficult Text

One article I used with students was on a topic that I suspected was unfamiliar to them—the debate on raising the nation's debt ceiling. Because of their unfamiliarity with the subject, I pretaught some of the concepts and vocabulary to them: *default*, *S&P*, *Dow Jones*. I also framed it by introducing Janet Yellen and took a couple of minutes to explain her role as the secretary of the Treasury.

---

20. You don't really understand the original *Planet of the Apes* until you get to the shocking reveal at the end of the movie. Until that point, you thought you understood the movie, but you didn't. For a more contemporary example, watch Jordan Peele's *Get Out*.

Doing this brief front-loading before students read the article positioned them to go much deeper with their reading. What we do before students read is critical.

Have Students Ask: What Did the Author Think I Already Knew?

If you have been in the classroom for even a short period of time, you will recognize this exchange:

> **Student:** I didn't understand the reading.
>
> **Teacher:** What part don't you get?
>
> **Student:** All of it.

When a student says, "All of it," what they are really saying is that they do not know how to monitor their comprehension. One way to move students past this is to ask a question I learned from Kylene Beers and Bob Probst (2016, 92): "What did the author think you already knew?"

Answering this question requires students to zoom in on very specific parts of the text to identify exactly where their comprehension breaks down. You cannot fix your comprehension until you know where it falters, and this question enables the reader to literally put her finger on the troublesome spots. I also like, as Beers and Probst write, how this question shifts the "blame" to the author rather than highlighting the students' lack of prior knowledge.

Teach Students to Avoid Clickbait

With so many online articles vying for our attention, we need to teach students how clickbait is used to draw them in. Start by teaching them the classic examples used to bait the reading hook listed in Figure 4–2.

On May 29, 2023, for example, I found the following headlines on the front page of CNN's website:

> See Beyonce's Surprising Backup Dancer During "Renaissance" Tour
>
> Doctors Are Warning of a Virus You've Likely Never Heard Of
>
> What's Killing Whales off the Northeast Coast?

Bait	**Example**
You'll never believe . . .	You'll never believe what happened to Taylor Swift after the concert.
X things you should know about . . .	Five things you need to know about traveling to Mexico
This weird trick . . .	This weird trick cut my weight by ten pounds in one month.
This is what happens if you . . .	This is what happens if you ignore the weather warnings.
Here are the *X* best . . .	Here are the seven best sunscreens.
X reasons why . . .	Ten reasons why the Angels will not win the World Series*
This is why . . .	This is why you should not swim in the ocean at night.
This is what . . .	This is what professional surfers do to train.
This is the . . .	This is the way to win your girlfriend's heart.
This is how . . .	This is how TikTok influencers become famous.
You can now . . .	You can now avoid paying much of your taxes.
The last . . . you'll ever need	The last hair dryer you'll ever need
Why you should . . .	Why you should stop watching the news
See . . .	See how to build muscle quickly.

Figure 4–2 Curry and Dourado (2023); Hennessey (2020)

* Actually, there is only one reason. His name is Arte Moreno.

Strange Occurrence in Venice's Grand Canal Has Authorities Stumped

These Are the Places Most at Risk from Record-Breaking Heat Waves as the Planet Warms

International Tipping: How to Cut Through the Chaos and Confusion

Europe Is Trying to Ditch Planes for Trains. Here's How That's Going

The 14 Comfiest Sandals for Women

10 Summer Appetizers You'll Want to Fill Up On

9 Delicious Recipes for Easy-Cleaning Cookouts

The 253 Best Memorial Day Sales to Shop Right Now!

The Best Electric Scooters in 2023, Tried and Tested!

Here Are the Best Deals on Apple Products

The Best Way to Cook a Steak Without a Grill

The Diet That Can Lower "Bad" Cholesterol

What to Know About Body Dysmorphia, the Condition Affecting Megan Fox[21]

And this is just one moment in time on one day! Once you've talked about the classic hooks, you might ask students to place these headlines in order of clickbait effectiveness, from most to least effective. Or you could ask them which one they find to be the most effective and to reflect on why the pull from this specific example is particularly strong. Once students understand how clickbait is used, have them select one new site and search it to see how many examples they can find (without clicking on the articles).

Earlier in the chapter I discussed how recognizing bias in headlines can help students navigate which articles to read and which articles not to read. The same is true in recognizing the propaganda techniques embedded in the creation of clickbait. Once students gain knowledge of these techniques, they can become much more discerning readers.

CLOSING THOUGHTS

Graduation at the end of every school year always stirred conflicting emotions in me—a mixture of excitement and concern.

Excitement because of students like Austin, who was curious and a voracious reader. He was armed with lots of knowledge and left high school with the capacity to understand, to question, to improve. He would not be a victim of an article being too smart for him, because if he got confused, he had developed a process to get out of trouble or had figured out where to turn to for help. Because he knew a lot, he learned a lot. He was the agent of his own learning.

21. This last example also employs the propaganda technique known as piggybacking, where a well-known figure (Megan Fox) is added to the bait ("What to know about . . .") (Hennessey 2020).

Concern because of students like Kolton, who years ago decided school was not for him. He *proudly* identified as a nonreader, and despite years of fake reading, he somehow made his way to the graduation stage. He left high school unarmed, unable to challenge complex reading. You have to know stuff to read stuff, and Kolton did not know a lot of stuff. He suffered from word poverty and, thus, idea poverty. I worried as I watched Kolton walk across the stage and accept his diploma.

Austin and Kolton were students of mine in the same English class. In the fall, you will receive a new batch of students, and within that group of students, you will find a wide range of reading abilities (and attitudes) in the Austin-to-Kolton range. While I couldn't do anything about the deficits my new students brought to class, I *could* start on day one and try to reestablish reading momentum as a means of filling their knowledge gaps. With reluctant readers like Kolton, this meant starting with interesting articles for them to read.

Articles are a great way to get reluctant readers started, but as I argue in the next chapter, there is an even richer resource for building prior knowledge: books.

WORKS CITED

Annenberg Public Policy Center of the University of Pennsylvania. 2022. "Americans' Civics Knowledge Drops on First Amendment and Branches of Government." Annenberg Public Policy Center of the University of Pennsylvania. September 13. https://www.annenbergpublicpolicycenter.org/americans-civics-knowledge-drops-on-first-amendment-and-branches-of-government/.

Beers, Kylene, and Robert E. Probst. 2016. *Reading Nonfiction: Notice and Note Stances, Signposts, and Strategies*. Portsmouth, NH: Heinemann.

Epner, Mitchell. 2023. "E. Jean Carroll's Lawyers Leveled a Knockout Blow on Trump." *The Daily Beast*. May 9. https://www.thedailybeast.com/e-jean-carrolls-lawyers-leveled-a-knockout-blow-on-trump.

Fanelli, James, and Corinne Ramey. 2023. "Donald Trump Found Liable for Defamation, Sexual Abuse in Civil Case." *The Wall Street Journal*, updated May 9. https://www.wsj.com/articles/donald-trump-found-liable-in-e-jean-carroll-civil-case-ordered-to-pay-5-million-for-sexual-abuse-and-defamation-25e175b9.

Gallagher, Kelly. 2009. *Readicide: How Schools Are Killing Reading and What You Can Do About It*. Portland, ME: Stenhouse.

Girish, Devika. 2020. "'The Social Dilemma' Review: Unplug and Run." *The New York Times*, September 9. https://www.nytimes.com/2020/09/09/movies/the-social-dilemma-review.html.

Grise, Chrisanne, and Lucia De Stefani. 2023. "A New Kind of Smoking Ban." *Upfront*, October 30.

Hennessey, Jason. 2024. "14 Surprising Examples of Clickbait Headlines That Work." *Search Engine Journal*. March 6. https://www.searchenginejournal.com/12-surprising-examples-of-clickbait-headlines-that-work/362688/#close.

Kittle, Penny, and Kelly Gallagher. 2021. *4 Essential Studies: Beliefs and Practices to Reclaim Student Agency*. Portsmouth, NH: Heinemann.

Krugman, Paul. 2023. "Wonking Out: International Money Madness Strikes Again." *The New York Times*, April 14. https://www.nytimes.com/2023/04/14/opinion/dollar-reserve-currency.html.

PoliTech. 2014. "Politically-Challenged: Texas Tech Edition." PoliTech, October 28. YouTube video, 3:07. https://www.youtube.com/watch?v=yRZZpk_9k8E.

———. 2016. "Politically-Challenged: George Mason University." PoliTech, February 10. YouTube video, 3:00. https://www.youtube.com/watch?v=I-t2TwLRdgk.

Revell, Eric. 2023. "IRS Plans to Hire Gun-Carrying Special Agents in All 50 States." Fox Business. April 27. https://www.foxbusiness.com/politics/irs-plans-hire-gun-carrying-special-agents-all-50-states.

Robelen, Erik W. 2011. "Most Students Lack Civics Proficiency on NAEP." *Education Week*, May 4. https://www.edweek.org/teaching-learning/most-students-lack-civics-proficiency-on-naep/2011/05.

Rui, Guilherme, and Shannon Hilson. 2023. "What Are Clickbait Headlines? [+ Clickbait Examples to Inspire]." *Rock Content*, May 22. rockcontent.com/blog/clickbait-examples/.

Singman, Brooke. 2023. "Trump to Appeal Verdict in E. Jean Carroll Civil Case, Says He Has 'Absolutely No Idea' Who She Is." Fox News. May 9. https://www.foxnews.com/politics/trump-to-appeal-verdict-in-e-jean-carroll-case-says-he-has-absolutely-no-idea-who-she-is.

Southern Poverty Law Center. n.d. "WorldNetDaily." SPLC. https://www.splcenter.org/fighting-hate/extremist-files/group/worldnetdaily.

Walther, Matthew. 2022. "Baseball Is Dying. The Government Should Take It Over." *The New York Times*, April 6. https://www.nytimes.com/2022/04/06/opinion/baseball-nationalize.html.

Wilson, Greg. 2022. "Watch: Fleccas' New Man-on-the-Street Video Captures Scary Big Apple Ignorance." *The Daily Wire*, June 3. https://www.dailywire.com/news/watch-fleccas-new-man-on-the-street-video-captures-scary-big-apple-ignorance.

Wolf, Maryanne. 2019. *Reader, Come Home: The Reading Brain in a Digital World*. New York: Harper.

5

Prior knowledge is foundational to moving students into "long" reading.

The Importance of Prior Knowledge AT THE BOOK LEVEL

Years ago, I was invited to participate in a book club discussion centered on Ana Castillo's *So Far from God*, a dazzling, multigenerational family saga. The meeting was held on the campus of UCLA, and there were going to be some prominent educators there, as well as the author herself. As a relatively new and unknown teacher, I was excited to be invited.

I arrived prepared. Well, overly prepared. I had flooded my copy of the novel with sticky notes, and when I walked into the room, I took my place at one of the thirty seats in a circle. My strategy was simple: I was going to let the conversation start to flow and then I was going to find just the right moment to interject a comment so brilliant that people would stop in their tracks and wonder, *Wow! Who is this guy?*

It wasn't long after the conversation started, however, that I started to feel uneasy. The novel centers on Sofia, a Chicana, and her four daughters, and the conversation began by discussing several cultural references that I did not fully grasp.[1] *Strike one!* (I looked around the circle of mostly Latinx participants and noticed I was one of a few Anglos as well as the only male.) The conversation then shifted to recognizing the nuances of the Spanish sprinkled throughout the novel, which went right over my head. *Strike two!* This was followed by a long conversation around the influence that Catholicism played in the development of the characters, and despite having the name Kelly Gallagher, I am not a Catholic and, thus, understood very little of the discussion. *Strike three!* Fortunately, I was wise enough to keep my mouth closed and simply listen to the wisdom in that room. In baseball terms, I was caught looking without ever swinging the bat!

I understood the book, but I did not *understand* the book. What was missing? Lots of prior knowledge.

☆–☆–☆

The *So Far from God* book club experience reminds me of the old adage that a book changes if you read it at different stages of your life. Take George Orwell's *1984*, for example. This book, a dystopian warning, resonated with readers when it was first published (1949), in the shadow of the totalitarian regimes of Hitler, Stalin, and Mussolini. I first read the book in high school when I was seventeen years old and then later went on to teach the book for twenty-five years. Every time I taught it, I understood it at a deeper level than the previous year as the world evolved and the predictions and warnings of Orwell eerily came to be. As I write this, it has been five years since I last taught the novel, but consider what has happened in the world since:

- Book bans have spread across the country. One district in Florida has even included dictionaries and encyclopedias in its review of "inappropriate" materials (Cohen 2024).
- A candidate for Missouri governor vowed to burn books if elected in 2024 (Bayless 2023).
- Deepfake technologies have improved, making it easy to spread incorrect information and propaganda. Concerns have arisen about how these technologies may be used to mislead voters (Klepper and Swensen 2023).

---

1. It would have been very helpful to have been well versed in telenovelas.

- AI is already being used to bombard politicians with concerns from their "constituents" (Shuham 2023). Millions of fake messages have already been sent.
- A news organization had to pay a $787 million defamation settlement for knowingly lying about election fraud in an attempt to discredit a fair election.
- A president of the United States lied or misled the public 30,573 times—503 times in one day (Kessler, Rizzo, and Kelly 2021)!
- Human writing is being replaced by AI-generated writing.
- Bots are being used to propagate bias and discrimination (Amos 2023).
- Our phones are listening to us—and this is legal (Stouffer 2023). (Yesterday, I went into a sporting goods store to buy some running shoes. They didn't have my size, so I did not make a purchase. An hour later, ads for those exact running shoes popped up in my social media feeds.)
- Whenever you use the internet, you leave a record of the websites you visit, along with each and every thing you click.[2]

If I were to read *1984* today, it would be at a deeper level than my reading just five years ago. The book did not change. My knowledge of the world did.

THE BENEFITS OF LONG READING

Maryanne Wolf, renowned cognitive neuroscientist, says that teachers and parents should strive to develop children who become "bi-literate" readers (2019, 170). By "bi-literate," she means readers who can critically navigate both click-and-go reading and book reading.

Anyone in a classroom today recognizes that click-and-go reading is supplanting book reading in the lives of adolescents. Fake reading of novels is occurring at an alarming level. In my workshops with teachers, I always ask, "How many of you suspect that many of your students are fake reading the assigned books?" It doesn't matter where I ask this question—the response is always nearly unanimous. (They often laugh at the question, as it has become rhetorical.) Students are not reading books at home, either. A recent study has found that only 14 percent of students read daily for

2. OK, this particular phenomenon is more than five years old, but it is still creepy.

pleasure, down from 27 percent less than ten years ago (Binkley 2023).[3] They are not reading books because they are on their phones or other devices.

A reading diet of strictly click-and-go reading is worrisome. Wolf wonders, "Will the time-consuming, cognitively demanding deep-reading processes atrophy or be gradually lost within a culture whose principal mediums advantage speed, immediacy, high levels of stimulation, multitasking, and large amounts of information?" (2019, 106–7). She worries that "many students who have cut their teeth on relatively effortless Internet access may not yet know how to think for themselves" (2010, 225). In an age of distraction addiction, students check their cell phones on average between 150 and 190 times a day and find themselves in what blogger Linda Stone calls "continuous partial attention" mode (2009). Worse, we touch our phones 2,617 times a day (Hari 2023, 20). Novelist Teddy Wayne adds, "Digital media trains us to be high-bandwidth consumers rather than meditative thinkers" (cited in Wolf 2019, 190).

What is an antidote to this pervasive hyper attention? Books. Holding on to your thinking over a three-hundred-page book requires a very different skill than click-and-go reading—a skill we should be aiming to restore in our young readers. Wolf advocates that readers need to develop a "quiet eye" to balance their hyper attention (2019, 69–71).

Beyond treating distraction addiction, reading books uniquely broadens our general knowledge. As cognitive scientist Daniel Willingham points out, "books expose children to more facts and to a broader vocabulary (a form of knowledge) than any other activity, and persuasive data indicate that people who read for pleasure enjoy cognitive benefits throughout their lifetime" (2021, 52). I recently read Quentin Tarantino's ruminations on 1970s movies, *Cinema Speculation*, and it introduced me to many films I had never seen (and now must see). Nick Bilton's *American Kingpin*, the true story of how a college student built a $1.6 billion dark website, Silk Road, where people bought any desired drug or weapon, describes a threat to our national security that I had never heard of. And reading Jeff Tweedy's *How to Write One Song* taught me . . . well . . . how to write one song. Reading these books broadened my knowledge, albeit in very different directions.

Books not only introduce us to new knowledge but also take us deeper into things we already know about. I understood totalitarianism, but I understood it at a much deeper level after I read Yeonmi Park's 288-page firsthand account of a harrowing

3. Postpandemic math scores have plunged as well.

escape from North Korea, *In Order to Live*. I knew the term *caste system*, but I didn't *truly* understand it until I read Isabel Wilkerson's *Caste: The Origins of Our Discontents*. I knew that stress can have negative effects on my physical well-being, but, again, I reached a much deeper understanding after reading Bessel van der Kolk's *The Body Keeps the Score: Brain, Mind, and Body in the Healing of Trauma*. And I thought I knew a lot about Martin Luther King Jr.—until I read Jonathan Eig's remarkable in-depth biography, *King: A Life*. There is a profundity found in these books—a depth not found in click-and-go reading. A deeper drilling down into areas where we previously possessed surface-level thinking.[4]

It would be a mistake to think this deepening of knowledge happens only through the reading of nonfiction. Fiction has enriched my understanding of several topics as well. Rebecca Makkai's *The Great Believers* taught me a lot about the AIDS crisis of the 1980s. Jodi Picoult and Jennifer Finney Boylan's *Mad Honey* opened my eyes to the transgender experience. Danya Kukafka's *Notes on an Execution* made me think about the death penalty in different ways, even though that was a topic I had been reflecting upon for years. Fiction not only deepens our understanding of topics but also develops skill sets we are trying to build in our students. As Christine Seifert notes in the *Harvard Business Review*, recent research in neuroscience has found that reading fiction helps develop "self-discipline, self-awareness, creative problem-solving, empathy, learning agility, adaptiveness, flexibility, positivity, rational judgment, generosity, and kindness" (2020). Reading fiction deepens our knowledge of the world, but doing so creates an added bonus: it deepens our understanding of what it means to be a good human being.

HOW TO HELP STUDENTS BUILD PRIOR KNOWLEDGE THROUGH READING BOOKS

Since books are the richest source in building prior knowledge, let's look at several moves teachers can make to enrich the reading experience.

4. This deepening of knowledge occurs on a professional level as well. I know a lot about the teaching of writing, but every time I read a Donald Murray book, I learn something new.

Restructure the Teaching of the Whole-Class Novel

One of my favorite poems is Wilfred Owen's (2018) "Dulce et Decorum Est," which captures the horrors of the Western Front during World War I.[5] In the poem, the narrator describes a gas attack and the image of a comrade who was unable to get his gas mask on in time. This haunts the narrator as he witnesses this tragedy unfold through the panes of his gas mask:

> ***Dim through the misty panes and thick green light,***
>
> ***As under a green sea, I saw him drowning.***
>
> ***In all my dreams before my helpless sight,***
>
> ***He plunges at me, guttering, choking, drowning. (29)***

One could read this poem and get an understanding of the horrors of the war. But I would argue that readers gain deeper meaning if they know the context in which it was created. Before composing this poem, Owen enlisted and was sent to the front line. During battle, he was caught in the blast of a trench mortar shell and spent several days unconscious, lying among the remains of his fellow soldiers. Eventually rescued and hospitalized, he was diagnosed with what was then called shell shock (PTSD is today's terms). While in the hospital, he suffered many nightmares, which inspired him to begin writing war poetry. One of several poems he wrote while hospitalized was "Dulce et Decorum Est."[6]

Knowing Owen's history and picturing him suffering from these horrific nightmares while hospitalized add a level of poignancy to one's reading of the poem. But, wait, the story does not end there. After Owen "recovered," he was given the option to return home; instead, he chose to return to the front, where he ended up leading numerous assaults on enemy positions. In one of these assaults, Owen was killed in action one week before the end of World War I. His parents received word of his death *on the very day that the war ended*.[7] The poem reads differently when we know that Owen

---

5. The Latin translation of the title is "It Is Sweet and Fitting." This is a shortened version of the last two lines of the poem: "Dulce et decorum est / pro patria mori" (29), which translates to "It is sweet and fitting / to die for one's country." The title is ironic—a searing indictment on those who used jingoistic slogans to lead a generation of young men to slaughter.

6. Among the other poems he wrote while recovering were "Anthem for Doomed Youth" and "Soldier's Dream," both of which are included in a number of modern anthologies.

7. Owen was largely unknown in his lifetime. He was posthumously awarded the Military Cross for his bravery. Most of his poems were published posthumously. Some scholars consider him to be the greatest World War I poet.

died a mere seven days before the armistice was signed. Even after I taught this poem for several years, knowing Owen's story led me to get a lump in my throat every time I revisited it.[8]

The notion that having prior knowledge leads the reader to gain deeper understanding is certainly true when it comes to reading novels as well. Recently, I read Julie Otsuka's *The Swimmers*, which delves into a mother's gradual descent into dementia. Here is the narrator describing a visit to her mother in a care facility:

> Every time you leave you bend over and give her a kiss. Sometimes she pulls away. Other times she looks at you and offers up an indifferent cheek. Always, as you are walking away—you can't help yourself—you turn around and look back. Sometimes she is watching you, but she doesn't seem to recognize your face. Sometimes she is gazing off into space. Sometimes she is leaning over in her wheelchair and staring down, intently, with fierce concentration, at the top of her feet. She has already forgotten you. Today, however, when you turn around and look back, her hand is half-raised in midair and slowly waving goodbye. (2023, 169)

If you've never had a loved one who suffered from dementia, perhaps this passage gives you a sense of what it is like. I say "a sense" because unless you have been there, you don't *understand* it. Reading this passage brought me back to my mother's memory care facility, and it stirred up several related memories of the last year of her life. It brought back the drip, drip, drip of losing someone you love. I lived it, and that experience brought a deep resonance to my reading of Otsuka's passage.

The value of possessing important prior knowledge has ramifications for how we structure our novel units. Think about the hardest book you teach—the one that keeps you up at night before the unit starts. I would surmise that one of the reasons that particular book is difficult for students is because it is far away from their prior knowledge. *The Great Gatsby* becomes a shallower reading experience if you enter the first chapter without knowledge of the Jazz Age or the mores of the Roaring Twenties. *The Grapes of Wrath* is a harder read without knowledge of the Great Depression or the Dust Bowl. *The Scarlet Letter* is more difficult if you enter into it without an

---

8. The source of Owen's biographical details is the *Oxford Dictionary of National Biography* (Stallworthy 2017).

understanding of seventeenth-century Puritanism. And so on. It's not necessarily the words on the page that make these books hard; it is the lack of prior knowledge.[9]

I learned this through many years of teaching Robert Louis Stevenson's *Dr. Jekyll and Mr. Hyde* (2022). When I first taught this classic, I began by planning the unit backward. I asked myself what I wanted my students to take from this reading experience. I decided I wanted them to consider the duality found in human beings, which is asserted when Jekyll states "that man is not truly one, but truly two" (70). Stevenson is suggesting that there is good in every bad person and bad in every good person, and I wanted my students to think about the nature of temptation and what that means in a modern context. (Early in the novella, Jekyll is in control of Hyde, but as the story progresses and Hyde increasingly finds pleasure in performing evil acts, Jekyll loses control. Over time, temptation overpowers him.) I wanted my students to get past the overly simplistic interpretation that humans are half good and half evil—to realize it is much more nuanced than that. This is a story of what can happen when you begin to give in to temptation and the internal conflict that arises. All of this wrapped in a tightly constructed murder mystery.

But here's the thing. When I taught the novella for the first time, I didn't teach it very well. It always took me three or four years—and sometimes longer—to refine any new novel unit. Some lessons were ditched; others, revised or created. There is a molding process around the teaching of any novel, and it was during this process that I realized the one area in which my *Jekyll and Hyde* unit fell short—*I wasn't front-loading it enough.*

I once heard Jeff Wilhelm say that the setting of a novel is not simply about the time and place of the characters but also about the time and place of the *author*. That is, to truly understand a book, you have to understand the context in which it was written. I learned this while teaching Stevenson's classic: a reader cannot deeply read *Dr. Jekyll and Mr. Hyde* without first understanding that it was written in Scotland during the Victorian Age. Because if you have any knowledge of what life was like in Scotland in the Victorian Age, this completely changes your reading experience.

First, the reading is deepened when one understands that the Victorian Age was a prudish time, a time of restraint. Reputation was of utmost importance—at least among the middle class—and this created a pressure to keep misbehavior under wraps. There was a marked decline in gambling, horse races, and risqué theatre. Too much sex was seen as unhealthy, and there was a sharp rise in prosecutions for sodomy. People kept things hidden. They were buttoned down, repressed—and this

9. Though, as discussed in Chapter 2, word poverty may also be at the root of the problem.

repression is key to the book. Dr. Jekyll is deeply repressed, and the pressure to not release his dark side is enormous. Eventually, the pressure blows and murder occurs.

Second, it is also helpful to know that this was written in an age where societal opposites were clashing. The book was published in the shadow of Charles Darwin's *The Origin of Species*, where new scientific thinking clashed with traditional religious beliefs. At this same time, men belonged in the public sphere, and women were primarily relegated to the private sphere. The author lived in Edinburgh, which was divided in two distinct parts: an old, crime-ridden medieval section inhabited by the poor, and the upscale side of town, literally on the other side of the railway tracks. Citizens of Edinburgh were also caught between the dual nationalities of Scotland and Great Britain, which created chasms across linguistic and religious lines (Campbell 2008). It is not an accident that Stevenson expertly wove in hundreds of hidden opposites throughout the book. (The first paragraph alone, which introduces the central character, Mr. Utterson—a "dreary yet lovable" man—contains seven opposites [1]. And that's just the first paragraph!)

Without an understanding of the Victorian Age and the context of living in Edinburgh, the reading of this classic murder mystery becomes superficial.[10] When you do possess this knowledge, however, you gain a much deeper understanding and appreciation of Stevenson's craft.

☆—☆—☆

What I learned by teaching *Dr. Jekyll and Mr. Hyde* was that I was not doing enough front-loading, a realization that led me to restructure the teaching of the other whole-class novels in my curriculum. When I taught Elie Wiesel's *Night*, for example, I had to provide more front-loading before the reading started, as not a single student knew the word *genocide*. To prepare them, we studied maps, charts, graphs, photographs, film clips, primary source documents, and firsthand accounts from Holocaust victims. This loading of background knowledge helped them connect with Wiesel's memoir. You have to know stuff to read stuff.

But there was much more to it than simply providing more background knowledge. Yes, students have to know stuff to read stuff, but even if they know stuff, they are still not going to read much, if anything, if they are not interested in the book. Teaching

10. Beyond these elements of prior knowledge, there is another layer of prior knowledge that deeply affects one's reading of this novella: the knowledge of different types of literary criticism. A reader approaching the novella through critical feminist theory is going to have a different reading experience than someone experiencing it through the lens of queer theory (the novella has very few female characters, and some scholars argue that Mr. Hyde is the embodiment of Dr. Jekyll's repressed homosexuality in an intolerant society).

Night taught me another lesson early in my career: we don't front-load just to provide necessary background knowledge; we also use it as a tool to generate motivation to read.

So how did I use prior knowledge to elevate my students' interest to read *Night*? I began by having them try to conceptualize the six million victims in ways that made it real. To get there, I started by sharing David M. Schwartz's children's picture book *How Much Is a Million?* (1993). When students realized it would take twenty-three days to count to a million, or nearly five months to count to six million, the numbers became more meaningful. And when they visualized that six million kids standing in a line four feet from one another would stretch all the way from Los Angeles to New York City, wrap around the Empire State Building, and then work its way almost all the way back to Los Angeles, the number became more than an abstraction.

From there, I asked students to consider where people congregate (e.g., a concert hall, a high school, Dodgers Stadium). I then asked them to solve a math problem: How many times would it take to fill up this venue before getting to six million people? Magnolia High School, where I taught, holds seventeen hundred students. This means it would have to be filled 3,529 times to reach the number of people who died in the Holocaust. Or to put it another way, you would have to fill up and empty our school *daily for almost ten years* to reach six million. This is a morbid activity, but when that number becomes real to students, they become more interested in reading the book.[11] I learned the importance prior knowledge plays in developing one's will to read.

There is a flip side to consider when planning a lesson around a whole-class novel: How much framing is too much? Is there a tipping point where more harm is done than good? I wanted to position my students to enter the book with enough background to make sense of the text. But if I gave them too much, I would weaken their ability to embrace and work through unfamiliar material. It is important, as Daniel Willingham notes, that we give students reading material that poses a modest challenge (2017, 143). I wanted them to discover thinking rather than have it handed to them. So how much framing is too much? And how much is not enough? It depends on many variables, and it takes experience to find the sweet spot with each book and each new set of students. When teaching *1984*, for example, I had to frame a lot. My students simply would not go on this reading journey with me if I asked them to read it cold. It was too distant and confusing. On the other hand, when I taught *Animal Farm*, I intentionally did not

11. One last thought about Elie Wiesel's *Night*. I read the book in high school and I understood it, but I understood it at a more visceral level many years later after walking the grounds of Dachau, one of the most notorious concentration camps.

frame the book at all. Instead, I told the students, "We are going to read a book about a bunch of talking animals on a farm, but—here is a hint—this book really is not about a bunch of talking animals on a farm. It's about something much bigger. Let's read it first and then we will try to figure it out." That's it. After they finished the book, I taught them about the Russian Revolution and the context in which Orwell wrote the novel. It was a lot of fun when students started making connections (e.g., "Hey, Napoleon is Stalin!"). I didn't give them this information before reading the novel because I wanted their initial reading to be *their* reading.

Teaching *Animal Farm* taught me that front-loading students with prior knowledge is not always a good thing. The word *novel* comes from the Latin word *novellus*, which means new or recent, and there were times in which I wanted my students' reading of a major work to be, well, novel. When we know too much about a book beforehand, it can dull the reading experience. (One of the challenges of teaching *Romeo and Juliet* is that almost every student knows how the play ends before reading it.[12]) There were times when I wanted the reading experience to be a surprise to my students. There is an excitement in traversing unmapped territory, of not knowing what lies ahead. Writer Walker Percy (2000) makes this point in his essay "The Loss of the Creature," where he considers the awe that Spanish explorer Garcia Lopez de Cárdenas must have felt when he became the first European to discover the Grand Canyon. One can only imagine the awe that overcame him after crossing miles of desert and breaking through endless mesquite to look down and find one of the seven wonders of the natural world at his feet. Today, a sightseer to the Grand Canyon has already seen countless images of it, and *that* Grand Canyon "is no longer the thing as it confronted the Spaniard; it is rather that which has already been formulated—by picture postcard, geography book, tourist folders, and the words *Grand Canyon*" (47). Knowing too much about the Grand Canyon dulls the edge of seeing it for the first time.

So when planning a novel study unit, prior knowledge is a tricky thing. My seniors who read *1984* and my freshmen who read *Animal Farm* both benefited from the teacher providing them with knowledge. But the first group needed this knowledge before reading the novel, while the second group benefited from acquiring the knowledge after completing the book. Deciding when, where, and how much you should support your readers—or whether you should support them at all—is where the art of teaching resides.[13]

12. When the blockbuster film *Titanic* was released, I had little interest in seeing it. I already knew how it was going to end.

13. It is also where the heart of my reading lies. When I pick up a new book to read, the first thing I do is read the overview found on the inside jacket cover (or online). I usually don't want to enter the reading experience cold (this is also true when picking my next movie on Netflix—I want to know what I am getting into). But not always. Sometimes it is more interesting not knowing anything. We have all had someone gush about a book we should read and found ourselves saying, "Whoa! Whoa! Stop! I don't want to know too much about the book." We yearn for the element of surprise.

☆-☆-☆

If we want to move students into long reading, we must also consider the relationship between prior knowledge and stamina. Students who are able to make connections while they are reading are far more likely to continue to read. Conversely, readers are quicker to abandon a book when it feels too distant or foreign. *Stamina is often directly influenced by one's prior knowledge.*

Once we have framed the novel and students are ready to read, we build stamina by abandoning the side-by-side approach to teaching novels. You know the side-by-side approach; it goes something like this: The teacher assigns Chapter 1 and then meets the students the next day with a quiz. The teacher assigns Chapter 2 and, again, greets the students the next day with another accountability check. And so on. The teacher remains side by side with the students as they progress through the book. This is problematic on a number of counts: it chops up the book so much that any reading momentum gets lost, the novel becomes an extended worksheet, and students are deprived of the necessary practice of reading beyond a chapter at a time.[14]

The alternative to this, as Penny Kittle and I describe in our work together, is to assign larger chunks for students to read. Instead of spending eight weeks reading the novel, our students were expected to read them in four. We would meet them only once a week, after they had read multiple chapters. Even then, we did not meet them with traditional reading quizzes. Instead, we asked our students to generate their own thinking and to bring this thinking to their weekly discussions. We were mindful that many students were leaving high school and then were unable to keep up with the reading demands awaiting them in college. Almost all reading in college is independent reading, and if students are not conditioned to read larger chunks before leaving twelfth grade, they are much more likely to drop out of college.[15]

Of course, starting the year by having students labor over a whole-class core novel is not the best way to approach the problems of fake reading and stamina. We build stamina through giving kids access to books they actually want to read and giving them time to read them (both inside and outside of class). In our year of teaching ninth grade together, Penny Kittle and I did not teach a core novel until the second quarter. We spent the first quarter building reading identity and momentum through

14. I write about moving away from this approach in greater detail in *Readicide* (2009).

15. The national college completion rate in 2023 was 62 percent (Spitalniak 2023).

lots of independent and book club reading.[16] Students had a lot of reading choices, another key element to building reading stamina.

It is important to teach students to monitor their stamina. I asked them early in the year to note how many minutes they were able to sustain their attention in uninterrupted reading. As the year progressed, we periodically repeated this monitoring. The stated goal: that students develop the ability to read and maintain their focus for an uninterrupted hour. And, of course, students who can sit and read for extended time will acquire more prior knowledge.

Teach Readers to Be Comfortable with Ambiguity

I started this book with a passage about the death of Colin Powell, and I considered the background knowledge that helped me understand it. But when we start reading a new novel, we often begin blindly. Consider, for example, the first paragraph of Erika L. Sánchez's *I Am Not Your Perfect Mexican Daughter*:

> **What surprised me most about seeing my dead sister is the lingering smirk on her face. Her pale lips are turned up ever so slightly, and someone has filled in her patchy eyebrows with a black pencil. The top half of her face is angry—likely she's ready to stab someone—and the bottom half is almost smug. This is not the Olga I knew. Olga was as meek and fragile as a baby bird. (2017, 1)**

One paragraph into the novel, and I am already swimming in confusion. Who is narrating? Is the narrator an older or younger sibling? Is she the only surviving sibling? How did Olga die? Where did she die? When did she die? Did anyone else die alongside Olga? Where is this story taking place? Is this a flashback or happening "now"? We are told that Olga's death doesn't make sense because she was meek—does this mean she stepped out of character and that doing so cost her her life? I simply do not have the knowledge to answer any of these questions.

---

16. Penny Kittle and I write about this in greater detail in both *180 Days* (Gallagher and Kittle 2018) and *4 Essential Studies* (Kittle and Gallagher 2021).

As an experienced reader, though, I do not default to panic mode. I know that if I hang in there long enough, the author will eventually clear up my confusion. I have learned to understand that confusion is normal—even for expert readers—and that living with ambiguity is not a bad thing. In fact, it is a part of reading that I really love. In this example, the reader does not learn how Olga died until several pages later, but I am patient because I know the reveal is coming. This does not distract from my reading. It propels me.

Many inexperienced readers do not know that confusion is normal. They get discouraged very easily if they don't understand everything at the outset. They have not developed the ability to live with ambiguity. To rectify this, I asked students to read only the first page in a novel and to list all the things that confused them. As they progressed through the novel, they periodically returned to their lists of confusion. As they got deeper into the novel, they could see that their early confusion had cleared.

Upon completion of the novel, I often asked them to identify an aha spot in the book—a place where their understanding shifted or snapped into place. (In *Dr. Jekyll and Mr. Hyde*, for example, the big twist is not revealed until the very end of the book. That's a long way to go without understanding what is really happening.) This means that when I asked students to write literary analysis essays, I shied away from questions that required them to analyze the work as a whole (e.g., What is the central theme of *Lord of the Flies*?). Instead, I might ask, "Where is a moment in the book where your comprehension shifted? How did the author achieve this surprise?" Answering this required students to revisit the text. As I discuss in *Deeper Reading* (2004), second-draft reading is often necessary to move beyond surface-level understanding. On a second-draft reading, students will notice new things. (When my students read the prologue to *Romeo and Juliet*, they were in survival mode, just trying to figure out what it said. It wasn't until their second-draft reading that they noticed the prologue was written as a sonnet. This realization came after wrestling with the meaning. They could not do both things at once.)

As I mentioned in Chapter 2, I want students to understand that comprehension is not simply a yes-or-no proposition. Reaching a deeper understanding of a novel means collecting fragments of knowledge and holding on to them until you can piece them together to make sense. This is why I worked hard to normalize confusion.[17]

---

17. Tom Newkirk, the editor of this book, suggests a hiking metaphor. Sometimes the trail is steep and you become winded easily, so you have to monitor your effort through the hard parts. After each hard part, you have to rest. This process helps you stay in control, being mindful to not become too winded. We should strive to instill this idea in readers confronted with difficult reading materials: Slow down. Hang in there during the hard parts. The trail will eventually even out.

Teach Students How to Retain Knowledge

It's one thing to understand what you are reading. It is another thing to remember what you are reading. One way to retain what you read is to write about it. When I read professional books, for example, I highlight key ideas. I do this quickly so as not to cause much disruption in my reading flow. Once I finish the book, I start a second lap, revisiting only the highlighted areas. I am searching for what Tom Newkirk refers to as "the sticky parts"—the big ideas that I want to stay with me (2017, 122). I write down these sticky parts in my writing notebook. In Figure 5–1, for example, are two pages in my notebook capturing big ideas found in Maja Wilson's excellent book *Reimagining Writing Assessment* (2018).

Note I did this writing by hand, because doing so offers "your brain feedback about the shape of letters in a way that keyboarding cannot, meaning writing by hand increases neural pathways for memory" (Tokuhama-Espinosa, Nazareno, and Rappleyee 2024, 48). This is supported by a number of studies, one of which found that students who took notes by hand learned and remembered more than students who took notes on a laptop. The researchers in that study found that taking notes on laptops led to "shallower processing" and a "tendency to transcribe lectures verbatim rather than processing information and reframing it in their own words" (Mueller and Oppenheimer 2014). Another study, published by *Harvard Health* (2012), even suggested that you will retain more if you do this writing just prior to going to sleep. This study resonates with me because I am a morning writer, and I have found that getting started in the morning is a lot easier if I write just one or two sentences before going to bed the previous evening.

You cannot use the same reading practices with all kinds of reading because the purpose for reading shifts. My purpose for reading professional books is different from my purpose for reading novels. In a professional book, I am trying to capture thinking that will help me become a better educator. When reading teacher books, I am already in a familiar world, but when I read a novel, my purpose shifts. I often *want* to be transported to an unfamiliar time and place. I want to *enjoy* the ride—to be carried away by what I am reading—and this pleasurable flow never occurs when I am forced to highlight countless passages or when I am required to stop after every chapter to answer another set of questions. My purpose is enjoyment and, if I am lucky, to exit the reading experience holding on to an interesting idea or two. Twenty years after high school, my students may not remember the names of Hamlet's childhood friends (Rosencrantz and Guildenstern), but I hope they retain thinking about the toxicity

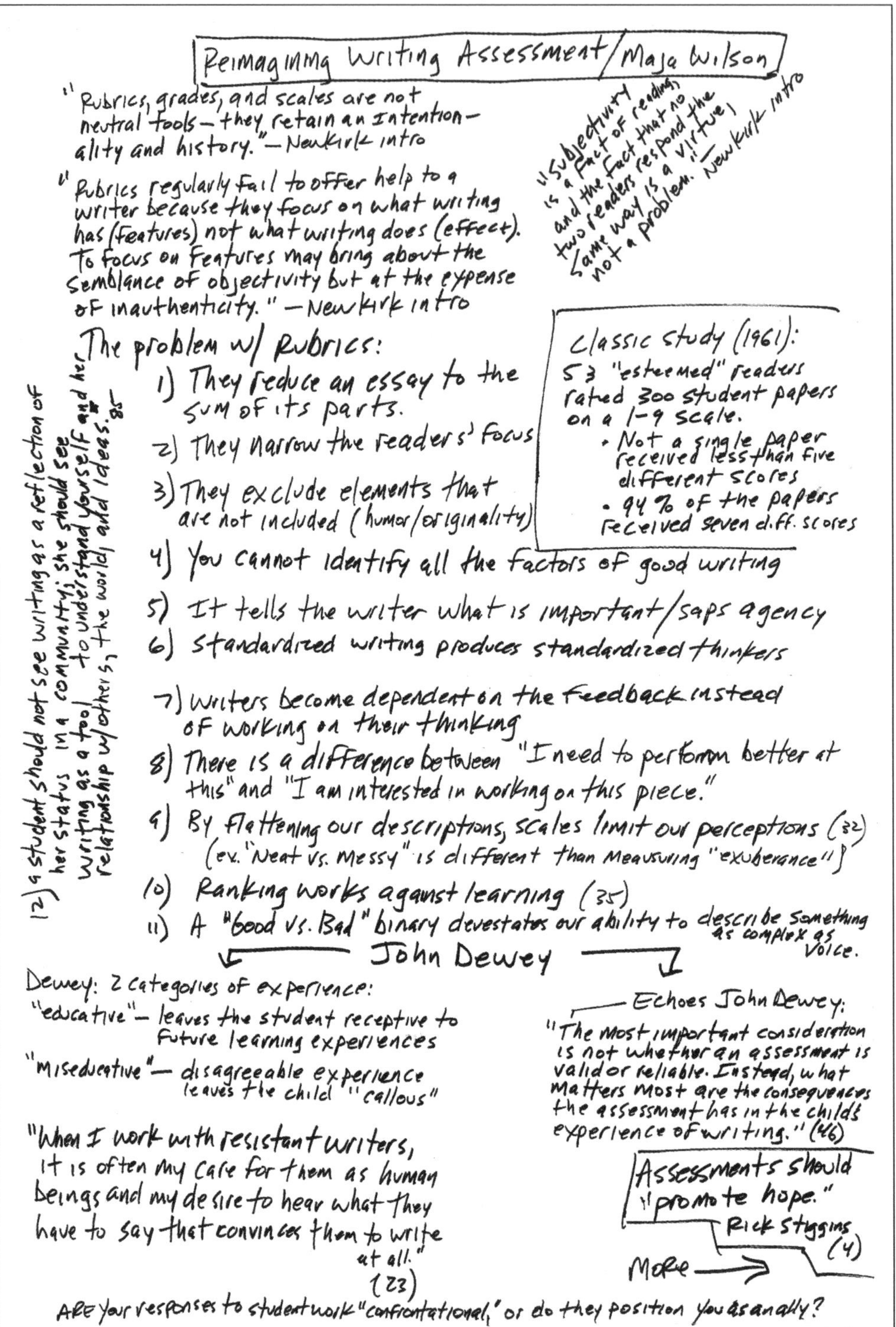

Reimagining Writing Assessment / Maja Wilson

"Rubrics, grades, and scales are not neutral tools—they retain an intentionality and history." —Newkirk intro

"Rubrics regularly fail to offer help to a writer because they focus on what writing has (features) not what writing does (effect). To focus on features may bring about the semblance of objectivity but at the expense of inauthenticity." —Newkirk intro

"Subjectivity is a fact of reading, and the fact that no two readers respond the same way is a virtue, not a problem." Newkirk intro

The problem w/ Rubrics:

1) They reduce an essay to the sum of its parts.
2) They narrow the readers' focus
3) They exclude elements that are not included (humor/originality)
4) You cannot identify all the factors of good writing
5) It tells the writer what is important/saps agency
6) standardized writing produces standardized thinkers
7) Writers become dependent on the feedback instead of working on their thinking
8) There is a difference between "I need to perform better at this" and "I am interested in working on this piece."
9) By flattening our descriptions, scales limit our perceptions (32) (ex. "Neat vs. Messy" is different than Measuring "exuberance")
10) Ranking works against learning (35)
11) A "Good vs. Bad" binary devestates our ability to describe something as complex as Voice.
12) a student should not see writing as a reflection of her status in a community; she should see writing as a tool to understand yourself and her relationship w/ others, the world, and ideas. 85

Classic Study (1961): 53 "esteemed" readers rated 300 student papers on a 1–9 scale.
- Not a single paper received less than five different scores
- 94% of the papers received seven diff. scores

John Dewey

Dewey: 2 categories of experience:
"educative"—leaves the student receptive to future learning experiences
"miseducative"—disagreeable experience leaves the child "callous"

Echoes John Dewey:
"The most important consideration is not whether an assessment is valid or reliable. Instead, what matters most are the consequences the assessment has in the child's experience of writing." (46)

"When I work with resistant writers, it is often my care for them as human beings and my desire to hear what they have to say that convinces them to write at all." (23)

"Assessments should promote hope." Rick Stiggins (4)

More →

Are your responses to student work "confrontational," or do they position you as an ally?

Figure 5–1

Maja Wilson —part 2 —

A claim that scores have grown is different than a claim that writing has grown, much less a claim the writer has grown. Research = conventions previously mastered tend to fall apart when students attend to more complicated grammatical structures, rhetorical situations, or genres. (50

"Has there been growth?" is different than "Has there been growth in the right direction?" (Dewey). (50)

The best assessment tools? conversations, observations, storytelling, interpretations → start w the student's intentions

→ to grow in the right direction, the student needs to be actively involved in the decisions that constitute the act of writing.

"Writing is a way of seeing and feeling and hearing, a way of asking and knowing, a way of creating and making sense, of expressing and communicating." —110

"The problem isn't the seed, in other words. The problem is that the environment isnt supporting the seed's growth" 135

Figure 5-1 *Continued*

of misogyny, the dangers of greed, or the pitfalls of revenge. Who cares if they don't remember why Marcellus insisted Horatio accompany him on his watch? As Dan Willingham notes, readers will forget much of any book they read. What is more important is that they retain the gist (2017, 107).

This raises many questions when sitting down to plan a unit around a major literary work. What is the ultimate goal? What is the gist? What are the one or two big things I want students to retain years from now? Thinking in terms of future retention helped me move away from planning lessons that overly focused on unimportant minutiae. I wanted a focus on the bigness of the book, and to get there, I wanted my students to acquire what Tom Newkirk calls a "feeling state"—that feeling you get when you recall a book (2017, 130). I remember very little about Anne Frank's diary, but I can tell you exactly what classroom I was sitting in when I read it the first time. I still carry—fifty years later!—the horror of what she experienced. As Newkirk (2017) notes, every book you read carries its own unique feeling. The feeling I carried from Anne Frank's diary is very different from the feeling I took from Ken Kesey's *One Flew over the Cuckoo's Nest.* The feeling I took from *Cuckoo's Nest* is different from the feeling I retained from reading Kazuo Ishiguro's *Klara and the Sun*. And so on.[18]

This focus on feeling state and bigness deeply influenced my unit planning. I still wanted my students to write—again, this writing helped them think more deeply about their reading—but instead of having them stop after every chapter to answer *my* questions, I required them to read much longer chunks before sitting down to capture *their* thinking. Instead of meeting them after fifteen pages, I met them after eighty-five pages, and I did not await them with a bunch of teacher-generated questions. Instead, I asked them, "You have read a significant chunk of this novel—what is worth thinking about thus far?" The writing I asked them to do was not task oriented. It was generative. I did not want them trying to spit out answers they thought would appease me. I wanted them to move away from extraction reading and to move toward the kind of writing that would help them discover their own thinking.[19] And if they captured this thinking in writing, they'd be more likely to retain it.

Encourage Students to Get into Other Reading Lanes

In Chapter 2, I briefly discussed the importance of moving readers into other reading lanes—that providing access to interesting books centered on unfamiliar people, places, and ideas is key to building a robust vocabulary. Diverse books expose readers to diverse words, and books often present these words in richer contexts than shorter reading experiences. But there are other, equally important reasons we want students to branch out. Maryanne Wolf, cognitive neuroscientist, notes, "The act of taking on the perspective and feelings of others is one of the most profound, insufficiently heralded contributions of the deep-reading processes" (2019, 42). Books, she adds, give us "the capacity to communicate and to feel with another without moving an inch" (2019, 43). This is no small goal for students coming of age in a deeply divisive and fragmented time.

There is a terrible irony here. On one hand, science tells us that one of the most profound things we can do to build deep prior knowledge is to provide access to

18. This idea of feeling state applies to movies as well. I don't remember much of the details of *When Harry Met Sally*, but I still clearly remember the infamous deli scene. If you know, you know.

19. In *Readicide*, I discuss the dangers of chopping novels up in greater detail. Penny Kittle and I also delve deeper into this idea in the two books we coauthored.

diverse books. On the other hand, there are numerous school districts that are actively *restricting* access to diverse books. Earlier in this chapter I discussed how Jodi Picoult and Jennifer Finney Boylan's *Mad Honey* opened my eyes to the transgender experience. But in the Martin County School District in Florida, *Mad Honey*—and dozens of other books from authors such as Toni Morrison and James Patterson—has been removed from classroom shelves in an effort to "protect" students (Susskind 2023). The irony here is that shielding students from diversity doesn't protect them; it *harms* them. Not only does it harm them by denying them reality, but it harms them because this restriction occurs while they are in a time of critical cognitive development, a time where they are much more receptive to understanding the world.

Unfortunately, the banning of *Mad Honey* is far from an isolated case. In the first half of the 2022–23 school year, there were 1,477 instances of individual books being banned, affecting 874 unique titles, this despite the fact that more than 70 percent of parents oppose school book banning (Meehan et al. 2023). The largest school district in Texas, the Houston Independent School District, announced some of its libraries would be eliminated and replaced with "discipline centers" in the 2023–24 school year (Walsh 2023). In Mississippi, a new law was passed in 2023 so that no one under the age of eighteen could have access to digital materials made available through public and school libraries without explicit parental or guardian permission—even though the age of consent in that state is sixteen (Jensen 2023).[20] "Even if granted parental permission, minors may not have materials available to them, if vendors do not ensure *every* item within their offerings meets the new, wide-reaching definition of 'obscenity' per the state" (Jensen 2023). Also in 2023, a judge in Florida ruled that classroom libraries can be severely restricted (Wong and Shah 2023). Other bans are occurring across the country, but they are more prevalent in Texas, Florida, Missouri, Utah, and South Carolina (Meehan et al. 2023).[21]

The movement to restrict books is gaining steam, and my heart aches for English teachers trying to instill the love of reading under this tyranny. I fear what Jodi Picoult warned us about will come true: she said, "Books bridge divides between people. Book bans create them" (in Sargent and Waldman 2023). Burning these bridges, bans will serve only to widen the divisions.

---

20. A female can legally get married at the age of fifteen in Mississippi but may not have full library access without parent permission.

21. Public libraries are under similar pressure. In 2022, "2,571 unique titles faced censorship attempts—a 38 percent increase over 2021" (Cowan 2023). "The library in Vinton, Iowa, found itself without any staff after librarians were reportedly harassed," and "the Patmos Library in Ottawa County, [Michigan], stands to lose funding in 2024 after a campaign driven by the presence of a handful of books on queer identities" (St. John 2023). And some conservative groups have promoted a "Hide the Pride" campaign, wherein they check out all of a library's LGBTQIA+-themed books and then hold on to them so no one else can access them (Cowan 2023).

Because of my concern with the rise of book banning, I approached Mike Matsuda, the superintendent of the Anaheim Union High School District, with an argument and a proposal. I argued that there needed to be a system—not simply a brave teacher or librarian—that took a public stand in favor of students having access to diverse books. My proposal, cocreated with my colleagues Penny Kittle and Taylor Kanzler, was to create a book club experience for students centered on diverse books that featured revolutionary characters. For the students in Anaheim, I selected the titles listed in Figure 5–2.

In the fall of 2023, students in California, Maine, and New Hampshire were placed in interschool book clubs. Students from each school read a different set of diverse books, and then they shared their thinking across schools. We need more of this kind of interaction between students and books.

Censorship is a denial of knowledge. If book banning is to be reversed, other organizations, legislative bodies, parents, and school districts will need to take stands. Fortunately, there are signs that the pendulum may be swinging back toward sanity. In Florida, the writers group PEN America, alongside the publisher Penguin Random House, filed a federal lawsuit over a Florida school district's removal of ten books about race and LGBTQIA+ identities, citing this as a violation of the First Amendment (Izaguirre 2023). In Illinois, the legislature passed a bill that prohibits libraries from banning books or other material because of parental pressure. Districts that cave to these pressures will lose state funding (Hancock 2023). And in San Diego, residents gave more than fifteen thousand dollars to a library to replace those books taken out of circulation by the "Hide the Pride" extremists. The city of San Diego matched this donation as well (Cowan 2023).

Teach Students That Some Hard Books Are Easy, and Some Easy Books Are Hard

A few years ago, my ninth graders were asked to participate in a book club, and one of the selections was Mark Fainaru-Wada and Steve Fainaru's *League of Denial*, a nonfiction account of the National Football League's attempt to whitewash the seriousness of brain injuries.[22] Four boys—all nonreaders—approached me and asked if they could

22. This book was made into the movie *Concussion*.

Title	Author	The Revolution
Two Boys Kissing	David Levithan	Harry and Craig, two seventeen-year-old boys, decide to fight homophobia by attempting to break the world record for the longest kiss.
Internment	Samira Ahmed	In this dystopia, Layla, a Muslim American, fights injustice after having been rounded up and placed in an internment camp.
Hollow Fires	Samira Ahmed	Safiya, a teenage journalist, works to get to the truth behind a hate-crime murder.
Last Night at the Telegraph Club	Melinda Lo	It's 1954, and two teenagers, Lily and Kathleen, fight homophobia in the shadow of the Red Scare.
The Firekeeper's Daughter	Angeline Boulley	Eighteen-year-old Daunis Fontaine, a member of the Ojibwe tribe, investigates a murder, and in doing so must choose between protecting the people she loves and protecting her tribal community.
We Are Not from Here	Jenny Torres Sanchez	Three teenagers, Pulga, Chico, and Pequena, flee the dangers of Guatemala and head on an epic, dangerous quest to find freedom.
How the Word Was Passed	Clint Smith	The author leads the reader on an unforgettable tour of monuments and landmarks—and shares some of the untold history behind them. (nonfiction)

Figure 5–2

read this book. My first thought was that it was too hard for them, but rather than immediately deny their request, I asked them to take the book home and read Chapter 1 before deciding if this was the right book for them.

The next day I asked them if they wanted to keep reading the book, and their answer was unanimous—they wanted to stay with it. Three of the boys ended up finishing the book. The fourth made it halfway. How were they able to read a book that was "too hard" for them? Two factors came into play: (1) All four of them were football fanatics and thus possessed a lot of prior knowledge about the topic at hand. They understood many of the references. (2) They were highly motivated to read, as they were football players concerned about their health.

Sometimes easy books are hard. If your football team is going to run the freeze option, for example, the center must smash the nose and block A gap back side. The offside tackle must ensure a gap seal hinge, while the slot receiver must either block nonprimary run support (option away) or block the inside number of the nearest DB. This is easy to understand if you are a football coach, but this becomes a very hard read for those lacking football knowledge—even if you understand each individual word.

In "Reading as Wedding Crashing," Tom Newkirk (2013) says that

> **a number of relatively 'simple' texts—for example, some of William Carlos Williams' poems—would be baffling to readers with no experience reading modern poetry. And, although many people find them daunting, I have little difficulty reading complex submissions to research journals because I have been reading them all my professional life. (Directions to our new widescreen TV are a very different matter.) So simple texts can be difficult, and complex texts can be easy—which is why reading-level formulas can only take us so far.**

Hand me a book about the Vietnam War, and I will have little trouble as I have already read extensively on the subject. Hand me a book on how automotive wiring and electrical systems work, and I will immediately exhibit the same reading avoidance strategies employed by nonreaders. I am a reader, but I do not have a reading level. I have several of them. If that is true for me, it is true for my students as well. Every student has several reading levels. We are all strong readers and we are all weak readers—it depends on what we are reading. Wrestling with hard reading in front of my students reinforces the idea that we never stop learning to read.

Teach Students That Understanding a Genre Helps You Read and Write in That Genre

When I sat down to write my first grant proposal, the first thing I did was find models of other proposals that had proven to be successful. I was unfamiliar with the genre, so I studied a stack of them. I wanted to get a sense of the rhythm of the language and to gain an understanding of what the parts looked like. I had to read slowly, as this type of reading material was unfamiliar. And when I eventually wrote my proposal, I often glanced back at the mentor texts for guidance.

Having experience in reading a genre helps one read and write in that genre. My friend Penny Kittle once suggested I write a crime novel. She knows this is my favorite genre and that I have read extensively in it. I know the DNA not only of the genre but of many of the subgenres. A Harlan Coben mystery has a different structure and rhythm than an S. A. Cosby mystery. When I sit down to read a Harry Bosch novel (written by Michael Connelly), I can anticipate that somewhere in the novel Harry will run afoul of bureaucratic roadblocks that will (temporarily) get in the way of his investigation. There is a strong likelihood that his daughter, Maddie, will be endangered. And somewhere in the book Harry will revisit the ongoing quest to find out who murdered his wife. Knowing these elements before reading the next book in the series is a *good* thing. Knowing the rhythm of the Bosch books makes them easier and more enjoyable to read. Reading widely across this genre has helped me hone a superpower: I am very good at figuring out the villain long before the reveal. (I am also adept at recognizing red herrings.) Because I have read so many novels in this genre, the reading is easy and comfortable for me. As a result, I am better positioned to try to write a crime novel. Maybe someday.

On the other hand, if you were to suggest I write a superhero novel, I wouldn't know where to begin. I have almost no experience with reading in this genre. I don't know the difference between a Marvel and a DC superhero. I couldn't tell an X-Man from an Avenger. While writing this paragraph, I googled "superhero movie tropes" and learned that Easter eggs are often hidden in these films. In *Suicide Squad*, for example, there is a brief glimpse of the Ostrander Building, which is named after John Ostrander, legendary author of several of the Suicide Squad comic books (Wynands n.d.). That would fly right over my head. Even if I were told there were Easter eggs sprinkled throughout the film, I'd never see them. I don't have the background knowledge to recognize them. And to think about writing a superhero book? No way. I don't know how this genre works.

Understanding how any genre works is a critical reading skill. A problem-solution essay has a certain text grammar, one that is very different from a reflective essay about a key moment in the writer's life. The parts of these two essays are different. Writing an analysis of *The Great Gatsby* is a very different task than writing a book review of Fitzgerald's novel. There are key functions of each genre that require the writer to recognize and name certain things. When you are well read in a specific genre, you develop an intuitive knowledge of these elements.

If we want to make reading accessible for students, we need to spend more time asking students how the text is constructed. In Chapter 2, I argued that understanding the construction of complex sentences helps students read and write complex sentences. The same is true of larger chunks of text as well. Understanding how essays, articles, and novels are constructed is the kind of prior knowledge that helps make the writing understandable. When students are reading a piece, have them collaboratively investigate the specific hallmarks of that genre. Ask them: "What did the writer do here? What did the writer do there?"

CLOSING THOUGHTS

It is helpful to think about when students adopt the identity of "I am not a reader." Why does that happen? What is the tipping point? When I interview nonreaders on why they stopped reading books, their answers often boil down to two key factors: will and skill. They don't want to read, or they don't have the skill to read. These two issues are related. When you stop reading, you fall further behind in your ability to read, and when you fall further behind in your ability to read, you lose the will to read. The reader gets trapped in a vicious reading death spiral. Reading becomes hard and boring—something you'd do only for school—and these are the students who found themselves in my twelfth-grade classroom unable to read *1984* even if they wanted to.

One of the reasons reading becomes boring to them is because they don't have a knowledge base that enables them to make interesting connections to what they are reading. Their disconnection reminds me of Bruce Ballenger's exercise "The Myth of the Boring Topic," in which he argues that there is no such thing as a boring topic (2001, 30). Ballenger has his students brainstorm topics they believe to be boring. He then teaches them to zoom in and critically examine their chosen topics. For example, a student might select dirt as a boring topic, but with a little digging (sorry), dirt becomes fascinating. One example: there are more soil microorganisms in a teaspoon of healthy soil than there are people on Earth (Cranmer 2018). The more knowledge you have about dirt, the more interesting dirt becomes. When students build knowledge, they are building bases of interest, which, in turn, builds confidence.[23] Conversely, less knowledge equals more resistance.

How do we crack this resistance to books? We might start by listening to David Sousa, a neuroscience expert, who reminds us that "how a person feels about a learning situation determines the amount of attention devoted to it. Emotions interact with reason to support or inhibit learning" (2001, 43). If students walk into our classroom with either a will- or skill-induced aversion to books, our first task is to change how they *feel* about books. This starts with surrounding them with lots of high-interest books from which they can *choose* and giving them time to rediscover the joy of reading without drowning their reading in quizzes and worksheets.[24] Sousa reminds us "that we need to be certain that today's curriculum contains connections to *their* past experiences, not just ours" (49)—which means finding books that *connect* to students' prior knowledge and backgrounds. This is *responsive* teaching. Once we have reestablished reading momentum and identity, and it comes time to plan a whole-class novel unit, we must carefully consider what students know, what they don't know, what they need to know, and when they need to know it. The answers to these questions determine when, where, and how we should frame the book.

There is a lot at stake in this quest to reestablish book reading. The United States has a college dropout rate of 40 percent (Bouchrika 2023), and one reason is that many incoming freshmen—who likely received As and Bs in middle and high school—cannot handle the reading demands of the university. As stated earlier in this chapter, almost all reading at the university level is independent reading, and many of these students have fake read their way through school. Their thinking has been replaced by online resources. When actually asked to read books on their own, many are not in reading shape. It is hard to run a marathon if you've never run a mile.

Beyond school lies a larger concern: What happens to a society that stops reading books? Pulitzer Prize–winning novelist Jane Smiley warns what might happen if books fall to the wayside:

> **My guess is that mere technology will not kill the novel. . . . But novels can be sidelined. . . . When that happens, our society will**

---

23. Researcher Maryanne Wolf says that books are uniquely positioned to help us develop a "widened eye" (2019, 88).

24. Penny Kittle and I discuss what this more balanced reading diet might look like in *180 Days* (Gallagher and Kittle 2018) and *4 Essential Studies* (Kittle and Gallagher 2021).

> **be brutalized and coarsened by people . . . who have no way of understanding us or each other. (cited in Wolf 2019, 53)**

Brutalized and coarsened. There is ample evidence of this in today's culture. Though the reading of books alone will not reverse this trend, it remains a critical piece in creating empathetic and thoughtful adults. As discussed throughout the first five chapters of this book, the building of prior knowledge is central to positioning students to be able to thoughtfully read sentences, passages, articles, and ultimately books.

Hopefully, lots of books.

WORKS CITED

Amos, Zac. 2023. "The Dangers of AI Chatbots—and How to Counter Them." Unite.AI. June 12. https://www.unite.ai/the-dangers-of-ai-chatbots-and-how-to-counter-them/.

Ballenger, Bruce P. 2001. *The Curious Researcher: A Guide to Writing Research Papers*. London: Allyn and Bacon.

Bayless, Kacen. 2023. "Republican Candidate for Missouri Governor Vows to Burn Books After Viral Flamethrower Video." *The Kansas City Star*, updated September 19. https://www.kansascity.com/news/politics-government/article279475914.html.

Binkley, Collin. 2023. "Math Scores Plunge for America's Thirteen-Year-Olds as Pandemic Setbacks Persist." *Los Angeles Times*, June 21. https://www.latimes.com/world-nation/story/2023-06-21/math-scores-plunge-for-americas-13-year-olds-as-pandemic-setbacks-persist.

Bouchrika, Imed. 2024. "College Dropout Rates: 2024 Statistics by Race, Gender, and Income." Research.com. June 6. https://research.com/universities-colleges/college-dropout-rates#2.

Campbell, James. 2008. "The Beast Within." *The Guardian*, December 12. https://www.theguardian.com/books/2008/dec/13/dr-jekyll-mr-hyde-stevenson.

Cohen, Li. 2024. "Florida School District Pulls Dictionaries and Encyclopedias as Part of 'Inappropriate' Content Review." CBS News. January 12. https://www.cbsnews.com/news/florida-school-district-pulls-dictionaries-and-encyclopedias-as-part-of-sexual-or-inappropriate-content-review/.

Cowan, Jill. 2023. "They Checked Out Pride Books in Protest. It Backfired." *The New York Times*, July 22, updated July 25. https://www.nytimes.com/2023/07/22/us/pride-books-library-protest.html.

Cranmer, Danielle. 2018. "7 Fascinating Facts About Soil." Rainforest Alliance. Last updated December 5. https://www.rainforest-alliance.org/everyday-actions/7-fascinating-facts-about-soil/.

Gallagher, Kelly. 2004. *Deeper Reading: Comprehending Challenging Texts, 4–12*. Portsmouth, NH: Stenhouse.

———. 2009. *Readicide: How Schools Are Killing Reading and What You Can Do About It*. Portland, ME: Stenhouse.

Gallagher, Kelly, and Penny Kittle. 2018. *180 Days: Two Teachers and the Quest to Engage and Empower Adolescents*. Portsmouth, NH: Heinemann.

Hancock, Peter. 2023. "Illinois House Passes Bill Prohibiting Libraries from Banning Books Due to Partisan Pressure." ABC 7 Chicago. March 22. https://abc7chicago.com/book-bans-illinois-library-house-of-representatives-politics/12993420/.

Hari, Johann. 2023. *Stolen Focus: Why You Can't Pay Attention—and How to Think Deeply Again*. New York: Crown.

Harvard Health. 2012. "Learning While You Sleep: Dream or Reality?" February 1. www.health.harvard.edu/staying-healthy/learning-while-you-sleep-dream-or-reality.

Izaguirre, Anthony. 2023. "PEN America, Penguin Random House Sue Florida School District over Book Bans." AP. May 17. https://apnews.com/article/desantis-book-bans-censorship-florida-5e648efdf241e333c9d5b042e65a7be6.

Jensen, Kelly. 2023. "Hoopla, Overdrive/Libby Now Banned for Those Under 18 in Mississippi." Book Riot. July 7. https://bookriot.com/hoopla-overdrive-libby-now-banned-for-those-under-18-in-mississippi/.

Kessler, Glenn, Salvador Rizzo, and Meg Kelly. 2021. "Trump's False or Misleading Claims Total 30,573 over 4 Years." *The Washington Post*, January 24. https://www.washingtonpost.com/politics/2021/01/24/trumps-false-or-misleading-claims-total-30573-over-four-years/.

Kittle, Penny, and Kelly Gallagher. 2021. *4 Essential Studies: Beliefs and Practices to Reclaim Student Agency*. Portsmouth, NH: Heinemann.

Klepper, David, and Ali Swenson. 2023. "AI Presents Political Peril for 2024 with Threat to Mislead Voters." AP. May 14. https://apnews.com/article/artificial-intelligence-misinformation-deepfakes-2024-election-trump-59fb51002661ac5290089060b3ae39a0.

Meehan, Kasey, Jonathan Friedman, Tasslyn Magnusson, and Sabrina Baêta. 2023. "Banned in the USA: State Laws Supercharge Book Suppression in Schools." PEN America. April 20. https://pen.org/report/banned-in-the-usa-state-laws-supercharge-book-suppression-in-schools/.

Mueller, Pam A., and David M. Oppenheimer. 2014. "The Pen Is Mightier than the Keyboard: Advantages of Longhand over Laptop Note Taking." *Psychological Science* 25 (6): 1159–68. https://linguistics.ucla.edu/people/hayes/Teaching/papers/MuellerAndOppenheimer2014OnTakingNotesByHand.pdf.

Newkirk, Thomas. 2013. "Reading as Wedding Crashing." *Educational Leadership* 71 (4): 44–48. https://www.ascd.org/el/articles/reading-as-wedding-crashing.

———. 2017. *Embarrassment: And the Emotional Underlife of Learning*. Portsmouth, NH: Heinemann.

Otsuka, Julie. 2023. *The Swimmers*. New York: Random House.

Owen, Wilfred. 2018. *The War Poems of Wilfred Owen*. New York: Vintage Classics.

Percy, Walker. 2000. "The Loss of the Creature." In *The Message in the Bottle: How Queer Man Is, How Queer Language Is, and What One Has to Do with the Other*, 46–65. New York: Picador.

Sánchez, Erika L. 2017. *I Am Not Your Perfect Mexican Daughter*. New York: Knopf.

Sargent, Greg, and Paul Waldman. 2023. "Ron Desantis's Book Ban Mania Targets Jodi Picoult—and She Hits Back." *The Washington Post*, March 10. https://www.washingtonpost.com/opinions/2023/03/10/ron-desantis-book-bans-martin-county-jodi-picoult/.

Schwartz, David M. 1993. *How Much Is a Million?* Illustrated by Steven Kellogg. New York: Mulberry Books.

Seifert, Christine. 2020. "The Case for Reading Fiction." *Harvard Business Review*, March 6. https://hbr.org/2020/03/the-case-for-reading-fiction.

Shuham, Matt. 2023. "Is America Ready for AI-Powered Politics?" HuffPost. June 22. https://www.huffpost.com/entry/artificial-intelligence-ai-astroturfing-influence-operations-propaganda_n_649495eee4b08f753c2aa4ee.

Spitalniak, Laura. 2023. "National College Completion Rate Stagnates at 62.2%, New Data Finds." Higher Ed Dive. November 30. https://www.highereddive.com/news/national-college-completion-rate-stagnates-at-622-new-data-finds/701061/.

Sousa, David A. 2001. *How the Brain Learns: A Classroom Teacher's Guide*. 2nd ed. Thousand Oaks, CA: Corwin.

Stallworthy, Jon. 2017. "Owen, Wilfred Edward Salter." *Oxford Dictionary of National Biography*. September 1. https://www.oxforddnb.com/display/10.1093/ref:odnb/9780198614128.001.0001/odnb-9780198614128-e-37828?sid.

Stevenson, Robert Louis. 2022. *Dr. Jekyll and Mr. Hyde: The Original 1886 Classic*. New York: Reader's Library Classics.

St. James, Emily. 2023. "I Am Being Pushed out of One of the Last Public Squares, the Library." *The New York Times*, July 17. https://www.nytimes.com/2023/07/17/opinion/public-libraries-book-bans-lgbt.html.

Stone, Linda. 2009. "Beyond Simple Multi-Tasking: Continuous Partial Attention." *Linda Stone* (blog), November 30. https://lindastone.net/2009/11/30/beyond-simple-multi-tasking-continuous-partial-attention/.

Stouffer, Clare. 2023. "Is My Phone Listening to Me? Yes, Here's Why and How to Stop It." Norton. June 13. https://us.norton.com/blog/how-to/is-my-phone-listening-to-me.

Susskind, Stephanie. 2023. "Dozens of Books Removed from Martin County Schools." WPTV. March 7. https://www.wptv.com/news/education/dozens-of-books-removed-from-martin-county-schools.

Tokuhama-Espinosa, Tracey, Jovi R. S. Nazareno, and Christopher Rappleye. 2024. *Writing, Thinking, and the Brain: How Neuroscience Can Improve Writing Instruction*. New York: Teachers College Press.

Walsh, Dominic Anthony. 2023. "Houston's Plan to Convert Some School Libraries into Discipline Centers Is Criticized." NPR. August 2. https://www.npr.org/2023/08/02/1191519700/houstons-plan-to-convert-some-school-libraries.

Willingham, Daniel T. 2017. *The Reading Mind: A Cognitive Approach to Understanding How the Mind Reads*. San Francisco: Jossey-Bass.

———. 2021. *Why Don't Students Like School? A Cognitive Scientist Answers Questions About How the Mind Works and What It Means for the Classroom*. San Francisco: Jossey-Bass.

Wilson, Maja. 2018. *Reimagining Writing Assessment: From Scales to Stories*. Portsmouth, NH: Heinemann.

Wolf, Maryanne. 2010. *Proust and the Squid: The Story and Science of the Reading Brain*. London: Icon Books.

———. 2019. *Reader, Come Home: The Reading Brain in a Digital World*. New York: Harper.

Wong, Alia, and Nirvi Shah. 2023. "Judge Sides with Florida in Challenge to Rules About Books in Schools." *USA Today*, July 7. https://www.usatoday.com/story/news/education/2023/07/07/florida-judge-tosses-teachers-challenge-on-school-book-rules/70391726007/.

Wynands, Michael. n.d. "Top 10 DC Movie Easter Eggs." WatchMojo.com. Accessed July 31, 2023. https://www.watchmojo.com/articles/top-10-dc-movie-easter-eggs.

One cannot think deeply without knowing a lot of stuff.

WHAT KNOWLEDGE? WHOSE KNOWLEDGE?

Implications for Teachers and Curricula

In the documentary series *Quarterback* (Dissinger, Furman, and Rumpff 2023), Minnesota Viking Kirk Cousins shares one of his favorite plays.

> **F-mode trick, cluster right tuna scram, X-steel, Y-cash, can it to Jacks, left cash, H-bronze.**

This is only one of approximately one hundred plays his team will select from their vast playbook for one week's game. But that is not all: Once that play is called in the huddle, then the quarterback must know what each of his ten teammates will be doing. After getting the team to the line of scrimmage, he must then read the defense. Is this the right play for this defensive alignment? Is the defense in man-to-man or zone coverage? Is a blitz coming and, if so, from where? Does the offense have the right protection scheme? Should it be changed? Or should he audibilize an entirely different play? Quarterbacks must make these decisions in a few seconds. And this is just one play. There will be seventy-five others called in the game. And that's just for *this* game. Next week's opponent will come in with a different defensive approach, so Cousins will have to learn a different batch of one hundred plays. You have to know stuff—a lot of it—to be an NFL quarterback. But this isn't true just about football. You have to know a lot of stuff to be a good pilot. A lawyer. A teacher. A bartender. And maybe more importantly, you have to know a lot of stuff to be a good citizen, a voter. *That we want our students to be knowers is not up for debate.*

So what should our students know? In the heat of the current-day battles taking place over curricula, we might start by remembering that the trouble created by trying to answer this question is not a new phenomenon. Americans have been arguing over what should be taught for many decades. Here are some of the most notable debates in the last hundred years:

- In 1925, high school teacher John T. Scopes was convicted of violating Tennessee law by teaching the concept of evolution in a public school.[1] This set off a curricular debate that still resides in some school districts almost a hundred years later.
- The civil rights movement of the 1950s and 1960s ushered in curricular revisions to include more lessons about racial segregation, discrimination, and inequality. These revisions were met—and are still met—with stiff opposition.
- The ethnic studies movement of the 1960s and 1970s advocated for more representation of diverse ethnic histories and cultures in the curriculum. This movement, too, was met with strong opposition.
- The Bilingual Education Act of 1968 was enacted, providing federal funding for those school districts that established programs for students with limited English proficiency. This set off years of tumultuous debate on how best to teach English language learners.
- Debates about sex education curriculum emerged in the 1960s and continue today.
- *A Nation at Risk* was published in 1983, setting off fierce debate on the best way to teach reading—a debate that also continues today.

1. Scopes was convicted, but the verdict was eventually overturned on a technicality.

- The No Child Left Behind Act of 2001 overemphasized standardized testing. This, in turn, narrowed the reading and writing curriculum and minimized or excluded subjects such as art, music, and physical education (as these subjects were not tested). These same concerns were repeated with the adoption of the Race to the Top initiative of 2009.
- In 2021, the Florida Department of Education announced that schools would not offer students the Advanced Placement (AP) African American Studies course unless the College Board (the creator of the course) removed "problematic" content (Cineas 2023). The course was then revised, omitting "concepts and scholars that experts, including many consulted by the College Board while developing the class, say are core to modern Black studies and essential to include in any college-level survey class" (Cineas 2023). State officials in Arkansas subsequently decided to offer the course but would not grant any credit toward graduation for those who took the class.

And the beat goes on. When I was a young teacher in the 1980s, my school district made the national news when our school board voted to ban Toni Morrison's *Beloved*, even though it was on the College Board's recommended reading list for AP literature.[2] I also recall that in that same time period, I walked out to my car after school one day only to be confronted by angry parents picketing on the sidewalk in front of the school. They carried placards that read, "Do you know your children read these words in class today?" followed by a list of out-of-context swear words culled from the novels on our core works lists.[3]

Today, when I hear people say curriculum has become political, I respond by saying curriculum has *always* been political. "All curriculum?" I have been asked. "What about math? How can numbers be political?" I answer by suggesting that how we count and what we count is very political. (I am reminded of the saying "There are three types of lies: lies, damn lies, and statistics."[4]) It would not take more than a minute or two to find an example online of how numbers are manipulated. When I google "How are statistics manipulated?" there are over twenty-eight million responses.

So, yes, all curriculum.

---

2. I don't think the school board appreciated it when I stood before them and sarcastically asked, "Perhaps you could recommend a happier book about slavery?"

3. Diane Ravitch's *The Language Police* is an in-depth look at the battle over words and how specific words and phrases become censored in American schools. She criticizes both the left and the right.

4. This phrase is often attributed to Ben Franklin or Mark Twain, but the origin is unclear.

WHAT SHOULD WE TEACH?

In 1998, E. D. Hirsch Jr., a professor of English at the University of Virginia, published *Cultural Literacy: What Every American Needs to Know*, in which he argued that American schools were focusing too much on the experiences of students and not enough on teaching "essential" knowledge. Hirsch advocated for a common body of knowledge to be taught, believing that a "national literacy" was critical to creating a society where people could read, write, and speak deeply to one another. If we don't share common knowledge, he argued, we won't be able to make these connections. Hirsch believed shared knowledge is the glue that keeps societies from falling apart. He noted studies that indicated a documented decline in shared knowledge, which coincided with lower literacy rates (5). Hirsch stated, "No modern society can hope to become a just society without a high level of universal literacy" (11). His keyword? *Universal.*[5]

Hirsch went further by defining what *specific* knowledge should be part of this universal literacy. To get all students on the same page—literally and figuratively—he published *The Dictionary of Cultural Literacy*, a collection of over five thousand things he believed all Americans should know, with sections ranging from the Bible to world geography to technology. He followed up with a series of books that defined what knowledge should be taught at each grade level (*What Your First Grader Needs to Know*, *What Your Second Grader Needs to Know*, and so forth all the way up the K–12 ladder). These contained sections such as "Language and Literature," "History and Geography," "Visual Arts," "Music," "Mathematics," and "Science."

Blowback to Hirsch's approach was immediate and vociferous. His ideas for the curricula were criticized for excluding diverse voices and perspectives and not taking into account the background and experiences of marginalized students. The concept of cultural literacy has been seen as "inherently conservative, excessively Eurocentric, intrinsically elitist and overly worshipful of archaic traditions. Worse yet, rather arbitrary lists of cultural literacies do indeed reduce education to an industrial-era emphasis on standardization and rote memorization" (Mintz 2022). Adopting Hirsch's approach, it has been argued, also limits students' opportunities to explore their own interests and passions.

5. This idea of a universal curriculum underlies the Common Core movement as well as reform in other countries. For example, the European Commission developed a new framework for quality learning (OECD 2020), which featured a set of eight competencies deemed critical for lifelong learning: literacy; multilingualism; numerical, scientific, and engineering skills; digital and technology-based competences; interpersonal skills and the ability to adopt new competences; active citizenship; and entrepreneurship.

Well, yes and no. Hirsch was not calling for a 100 percent common curriculum. He advocated for a split: 40 percent to 60 percent of a common curriculum, with the remainder open to local and regional decisions. (In California, for example, all fourth graders study the history around the California missions. In New England, there is a heavier emphasis on early Colonial history, while students living in the Great Plains study the Dust Bowl and the history of indigenous peoples.) Hirsch argued that it was imperative that a large portion of the curriculum centered on acquiring shared knowledge and that the earlier this acquisition started, the better. He cited the education system in France, where 98 percent of children are enrolled in state-sponsored preschool with a common curriculum. Some French children start preschool as early as the age of two, and studies have shown that the earlier a student starts school, the more likely they are to become excellent readers. This is especially true of students who come from disadvantaged backgrounds. Because they start early, the powerful Matthew effect (the rich get richer) works for them, not against them.

I wrestled with a 100 percent–mandated reading curriculum early in my career. Back then, all English teachers in my district were required to teach the same core novels and plays chosen from a short list of canonical titles written primarily by white, male authors. No choice. No deviation. Any suggestion of revising the list to include diverse and contemporary books was met with fierce opposition by the old guard, who saw these proposals as a blasphemous watering down of the curriculum. *The Scarlet Letter* would have to be pried from their cold, dead fingers. Over time, however, this rigidness began to thaw, largely driven by student indifference and disengagement. But it was also directed by a small group of teachers who saw the mandated list as a form of hegemony, that this disengagement was largely centered on a curriculum that ignored the rich cultural backgrounds of our students, and, worse, that this disengagement *ensured* that these students would remain marginalized.

My students were largely Latinx, and the mandated tenth-grade curriculum required them to read *Lord of the Flies*, *Fahrenheit 451*, *A Separate Peace*, *To Kill a Mockingbird*, and *Farewell to Manzanar*. With this imbalance in mind, I proposed that the district adopt Rudolpho Anaya's *Bless Me, Ultima*. (I wanted to pair it with *To Kill a Mockingbird*, as both books explore big ideas: racism, justice, coming of age, morality.) Yes, adding *Bless Me, Ultima* meant subtracting one of the entrenched titles, but I knew my students would connect culturally to the richness of Anaya's novel. This was a small compromise, which the district eventually agreed to.

Flash forward thirty years, and my students read a wide range of writers across numerous cultures (as evidenced by some of the selections mentioned in the last chapter). Instead of reading six major literary works in lockstep, my students and I read two core texts together—one each semester. There is a value in reading a core text together—a value not found when reading individually or in small groups. The rest of the year, they were free to select books they wanted to read (either independently or in book clubs) because there is also a value that arises when students develop allegiances to authors they have chosen. Both of these values can be true.

☆-☆-☆

Before we can consider what we should teach, let's review some big ideas about curricula. Specifically, any given curriculum should

arise from a collaborative process;

be balanced and structured;

strike a balance between depth and breadth;

lead to tuned-in teaching; and

be more than meets the eye.

THE CURRICULUM SHOULD ARISE FROM A COLLABORATIVE PROCESS

In "What Every American Should Know," Eric Liu (2015) argues that our goal should be to create a common culture that's greater than the sum of our increasingly diverse parts:

> **It's not enough for the United States to be a neutral zone where a million little niches of identity might flourish; in order to make our diversity a true asset, Americans need those niches to be able to share a vocabulary. Americans need to be able to have a broad base of common knowledge so that diversity can be most fully activated.**

The list, quite simply, must be the mirror for a new America. As more diverse voices attain ever more forms of reach and power we need to re-integrate and reimagine Hirsch's list of what literate Americans ought to know.

What we teach should be decided by diverse voices of stakeholders. We might start, as Liu suggests, by having teachers in each content area list ten things every student should know in each course. If I were to teach a government class, for example, here would be my list:

the US Constitution

the Bill of Rights

the three branches of government—checks and balances

federalism versus states' rights

the electoral college

gerrymandering

voter suppression

veto

filibuster

lobbying

The lists from other social studies teachers would certainly differ, but I am reminded of a phrase that has often been attributed to Howard Zinn, author of *A People's History of the United States*: "History without discomfort is propaganda." Through a process of aggregation and discussion, eventually a crowd-sourced list of what we should teach could emerge. We should use this same process to decide what we want students to read. Doing so would surely raise some interesting questions: What should the balance be between shorter pieces (articles, short stories) and full-length books? What should be the ratio of fiction to nonfiction? And maybe most importantly, *whom* should students be reading?

What Authors Should Students Be Reading?

The question of which authors students should read raises an interesting issue. Take J. K. Rowling, for example. Recently, there has been a movement to cancel her because of comments she made that many consider to be transphobic. Does that mean our students should no longer read the Harry Potter series? To answer this question, consider this story of Cat Stevens, one of the most successful singer-songwriters of the 1970s. I love his music, but I boycotted it for thirty years. Why? Because Stevens, who changed his name to Yusuf Islam upon converting to Islam, publicly endorsed the notion of killing the author Salman Rushdie because he believed Rushdie's book *The Satanic Verses* to be blasphemous.[6] When I learned this, I stopped listening to his music.

But was I right to do so? My thinking has shifted since reading Claire Dederer's *Monsters: A Fan's Dilemma* (2023). Dederer explores the dilemma that many fans are faced with today: Should an artist—like Cat Stevens or J. K. Rowling—be canceled for exhibiting reprehensible behavior? How are we to experience art when we are morally outraged with the artist? Although she does not take a definitive stance, Dederer warns that cancellation of these artists leads to a slippery slope. If we are to take a moral stand against wrongdoers, does this mean we can no longer appreciate their art? Do we stop watching the films of Woody Allen or Roman Polanski? Should we stop listening to the music of Miles Davis or Michael Jackson? Should the paintings of Picasso and others be removed from museums? All of these are "monstrous" people. Does their behavior mean we should ignore their art? Is it the art, or is it the artist?

This is a question I've had to wrestle with while planning my reading curriculum. For years, I used a Sherman Alexie passage to teach voice, sensory detail, and dialogue. But when Alexie apologized amid allegations of sexual misconduct, I pulled his work from my classroom. I used another passage from Junot Díaz to teach students imitation before learning he, too, was accused of unwanted sexual advances. I pulled that lesson, too. But was I right to do so? Should I also pull *The Maze Runner* from my classroom library because James Dasher, the author, has faced accusations of sexual harassment? And if *The Maze Runner* goes, do I also need to pull *Thirteen Reasons Why*? (Jay Asher, the author, has also faced similar accusations.) Is reading Ernest Hemingway or Norman Mailer now out-of-bounds? Where do we draw the line?

It's a little scary sharing this publicly—because some readers will disagree with me—but reading Dederer's book has moved me back to the "It's the art, not the artist" side. I now listen to Cat Stevens again. And if I were in the classroom today, I would keep *The Maze Runner* and *Thirteen Reasons Why* in my classroom library. When planning your students' reading pathway, there are difficult decisions you may have to make when your knowledge leads to morally tricky questions. Is it the art? Or is it the artist?

---

6. In 2022, Rushdie was stabbed several times while giving a speech in Chautauqua, New York. He was gravely injured but survived. Irony: one of Stevens' most popular songs is "Peace Train."

That is a lot to think about when planning your students' reading journey. I'd like to add one more consideration: Given the climate and battles over students' access to diverse books, it is likely that someone will try to impose *their* personal beliefs on *all* of your students. One common rationale behind book banning, for example, is that a particular book is too disturbing for young readers. To counter this notion, consider a four-year study of over four hundred adolescent readers conducted by Gay Ivey and Peter Johnston (2023). They found that rather than harming children, "disturbing" books were central to building social, emotional, and intellectual growth:

> **Students described characters' questionable decisions as cautionary tales, not narratives to live into, a concept they found laughable, plausible only to someone who hadn't read the book. The books helped them to see the consequences of problematic decisions and language. . . . The complexities of characters' lives and the consequences of their decisions deepened students' moral thinking while making them grateful for their lives and families. The books reduced their own self-absorption, diminishing personal concerns that might otherwise overwhelm them. Bad words and disturbing scenes simply fed bigger conversations about life and relationships.**

And as part of the collaborative process in picking diverse books,[7] let us not forget to include librarians, whose expertise is invaluable.[8]

THE CURRICULUM SHOULD BE BALANCED AND STRUCTURED

One of the negative effects of the Common Core State Standards is that the testing overvalued ELA and math classes while undervaluing other content areas. As a result, less time was devoted to teaching topics other than language arts and math. This imbalance was evident even before the implementation of

7. This is what teachers in my school district did to create the list of titles found in Figure 2–2.

8. As I write this, there is a glimmer of hope for librarians who are under fire. Some librarians who were fired in the culture wars have filed workplace discrimination claims with the US Equal Employment Opportunity Commission (Gruver 2023). Whether this will work or not remains to be seen.

these new standards, as cited in one study that found that in the height of the testing madness, second graders spent two hours and five minutes a day studying language arts and math and only eight minutes a day learning other academic subjects (Rosenshine 2015). Fifth graders were found to have a similar curricular imbalance, spending two hours and thirty-five minutes daily studying language arts and math while devoting only seventeen minutes a day to other content areas. There is an irony here, as much of the reading passages on high-stakes exams involve history and science. Students with broad knowledge of content area words and concepts are at a distinct advantage when taking these exams, which is why many have called for more time and attention to subjects other than math and English.

One way of ensuring we achieve that balance is by making sure a structured reading curriculum is in place. This sounds simple, but as Schmoker and Marzano (1999) note, "curricular chaos" is prevalent in many school systems.[9] Linda Darling-Hammond, professor of education emeritus at Stanford University, studied three high-performing countries (Finland, Singapore, and South Korea) and found that they share three common characteristics: they have equally well-resourced schools, they benefit from uniformly well-prepared teachers, and they *learn the same core content (within their respective countries)* (in Walker 2017; italics mine). Unfortunately, many school systems in the United States fall short of at least one, if not all, of these factors.

Let's be clear. By "structure," I am not advocating that English teachers teach the same page of the same chapter of the same novel on the same day. Rather, teachers (and students) should have a map of when and where they are going. In my collaboration with Penny Kittle (2018), I created a reading map for my twelfth graders (see Figure 6–1).[10]

Our senior teachers all taught *Hamlet* in the same month, but *how* they taught the play was up to each individual teacher (though we did collaborate extensively on which standards we'd teach in each unit). Outside of the core works, students had a lot of choice on what to read in book clubs, but all students were in book clubs at the same time.

Having this reading map in front of me as the year started was very helpful. It reminded me that students need a balanced reading diet. In the mayhem of the school year, it is easy to drift offtrack, but having this map—and knowing that my colleagues were following this map—was helpful in making sure I did not veer too far away from what was deemed essential.

---

9. Though Schmoker and Marzano wrote of the problem of curriculum chaos in 1999, Schmoker indicated in a recent conversation that the problem still persists today.

10. Penny Kittle and I also created a writing map in *180 Days*.

Weeks	Ending	Work
1–4	9/13	Free choice: independent reading
5–8	9/27	Book club 1
9–14	11/8	Free choice: independent reading
15–19	12/20	Core work: *Hamlet*
Semester break		
20–23	1/31	Book club 2
24–27	3/6	Free choice: independent reading or book club
28–32	4/10	Core work: *1984*
32–35	5/1	Book club 3

Figure 6–1

And it is easy to veer. It is also easy to drown. When planning curriculum maps, we must begin by recognizing that it would take twenty-two years of schooling to adequately teach the K–12 standards (Marzano 2003, 26–27). There are simply too many standards, too many students, and not enough time to teach. Prioritization is the first step, and we begin by identifying what Doug Reeves (2021) calls the "power standards"—the subset of standards that are most important for your students to be successful. Hard decisions must be made. What will we teach? What will we leave out? Is this lesson worth the time? Mike Schmoker (2020) has argued that less is more and that our students' literacy would soar if we focused on only five key questions:

1. How many books, articles, poems, and textbook excerpts have students read?
2. How many pages have students read?
3. How much informal writing have students produced?
4. How many formal papers have students produced?
5. How many meaningful conversations (e.g., Socratic seminars) have students had?

Schmoker's first two questions—How many pages have students read? How many books have students read?—are also important reminders to not get lost in the standards weeds (more on this soon). You can teach every reading standard, but it will not matter if kids are not reading. Marzano and Kendall (1998) studied the various factors that impact student achievement. The number one factor? That students have an "opportunity to learn" via a "guaranteed and viable curriculum" (Marzano 2003, 22). Are we giving our students an opportunity to actually read?

THE CURRICULUM SHOULD STRIKE A BALANCE BETWEEN DEPTH AND BREADTH

To learn something deeply means spending more time on a topic or subject. But spending more time on a topic or subject also means students will spend less time on the curriculum as a whole. In our attempt to build as much prior knowledge as possible, how do we reconcile this dilemma? How do we balance depth and breadth?

The answer lies in the middle. Hirsch notes, "We cannot gain deep understanding without having broad factual knowledge. On the other hand, piling up more and more facts that don't really add much to our understanding or ability to learn wastes our time" (2001). Hirsch advocates for a curriculum that teaches a diversity of topics (science, history, ethics, literature, and the arts), not just the formal skills of reading, writing, and arithmetic. In doing so, "we should also teach in some depth a moderate number of specific examples" (2001). When applied to the reading curriculum, this means students should be reading assignments like the article of the week while also reading books. Our first goal is to get students to get into reading lanes, and once they have established some momentum as readers, it is time to guide them into other reading lanes.

When there are too many reading standards to teach, which ones should move to the front of the line? Reeves (2021) suggests identifying "power standards"—standards that meet three criteria: endurance, leverage, and necessity for the next level of instruction. Take, for example, the ability to read charts. We can teach this skill across all grade levels (endurance), we can teach it in more than one content area (leverage), and students need it as they encounter increasingly challenging charts as they get older (necessity for the next level of instruction) (2021). It is power standards like this that should have precedence.

Deciding what to teach is getting harder. Every year, it seems, the curriculum grows. Teaching students how to ethically and intelligently read and use chatbots and other AI platforms is imperative—a unit that did not exist a short time ago. If we add this, then something else must go (as was the case when my district adopted *Bless Me, Ultima*). So who should make these difficult choices? Reeves notes, "I would not expect any state or provincial jurisdiction to identify power standards, because the political pressures at the state level are for coverage. *Only schools and districts can make the tough choices* to say out loud what we all know to be true—not every standard is important, and there are too many standards for the time we have available in the classroom" (2021; italics mine). This also means moving away from having students read only short passages and moving them into book reading. Making these decisions is an act of courage, as they often fly in the face of testing pressures.

THE CURRICULUM SHOULD BE TUNED IN—A LIVING, BREATHING THING

The chatbot example in the previous paragraph is a reminder that the curriculum is a living, breathing thing. Our students are continually changing, and the curriculum should as well. We want to ensure that our teaching is tuned in so that students sitting in our classrooms are engaged and that what we teach them will have an immediate impact on their lives (Garcia and Morrell 2022). This means moving away from the factory model of schooling that has roots all the way back to the early nineteenth century.

What do I mean by having a curriculum that is tuned in to our students? It is not uncommon, for example, for students in English classes to write one literary analysis essay after another—this despite the fact that only 2.8 percent of college students are English majors (Phelps 2023). This is the opposite of being tuned in. As Penny Kittle and I have argued (2022), wouldn't it be better to remove one of these essays and replace it with a digital composition? Shouldn't we honor the expertise students bring with them to class? On the reading side, wouldn't it be better to update the reading lists so students have access to diverse, high-interest books? If a core text is too difficult for most of the students in the class, should we just plow forward and continue teaching it simply because that is the way it has always been? What is in the best interest of the students?[11]

As I'm writing this, the Anaheim Union High School District—my home for thirty-five years—is believed to be the first school district in the United States to offer a course in Korean studies. This course was created as a response to rising anti-Asian hate crimes, both locally and nationally. Nearly 20 percent of the district's student population are Asian Pacific Islanders, and the district felt it was important to address their collective history and affirm individual identities in the context of American history and the civil rights struggle. In this and other ethnic studies courses, the approach is to gain appreciation of others by reading personal and generational narratives and storytelling. In Anaheim, the curriculum is evolving to help students stay tuned in. The curriculum is *responsive* to the students sitting in the classrooms.

THE CURRICULUM IS MORE THAN MEETS THE EYE

The word *curriculum* as it is defined from its early Latin origins means literally "to run a course." But given the complexity of schools today, that definition seems too narrow. I like Tom Vander Ark's[12] idea that curriculum is "a sequence of mental, physical and emotional experiences. That definition keeps the focus on the experience of the learner" (2017). These mental, physical, and emotional experiences go far beyond any single lesson or unit plan.

Here's an example of an emotional experience that went beyond my lesson of the day. I was in the middle of reading something with my students when the campus security guard walked into my room, interrupted me midsentence, and called for a student to be removed. The student, obviously in some sort of trouble, stood up, embarrassed, and grumbled as he shuffled toward the door. Impatient, the security guard rolled her eyes and sarcastically said, "I'm sure you were deeply engaged in this scintillating lesson. Let's go."

I was stunned. Her comments sent a powerful message to *all* the students in the room that this student wasn't a worthy learner, that learning rarely happens at this

---

11. What is best for teachers is not always what is best for the students.

12. Vander Ark is the author of several books on how to improve schools.

school, and that I was nothing more than a glorified babysitter. After class, I tracked down the security guard and said, "Just so you know, that *was* a scintillating lesson and that student *was* engaged. I am not always successful by any means, but I aim for a scintillating lesson *every single day.*" The color drained from the security guard's face as she profusely apologized.

The security guard incident reminds me of Leslie Owen Wilson's (n.d.) notion that "since students learn all the time through exposure and modeled behaviors, this means that they learn important social and emotional lessons from everyone who inhabits a school—from the janitorial staff, the secretary, the cafeteria workers, their peers, as well as from the deportment, conduct, and attitudes expressed and modeled by their teachers. Many educators are unaware of the strong lessons imparted to youth by these everyday contacts." These everyday contacts are critical. This is why I greeted my students at the door every day. This is why I had boxes of energy bars and other snacks in the back of my classroom for my students to freely access.[13] This is why the first thing you noticed when walking into my room was the extent of my classroom library. All part of the curriculum. All helpful in advancing learning.

There is even more to the traditional curriculum than meets the eye—but not in a good way. Take AP classes, for example. AP exams drive a very narrow, inauthentic form of reading and writing. And because teachers who teach AP classes are judged by their students' scores on these exams, this narrow, inauthentic reading and writing is what they teach. This concern is shared by Annie Abrams, author of *Shortchanged: How Advanced Placement Cheats Students*, who notes,

> More than ever, AP essays measure a basic ability to conform and regurgitate, not the cultivation of subjectivity nor a meaningful understanding of the writing process. Importantly, the new rubrics also restrict graders from making qualitative judgments that require knowledge and trust.[14] The drive toward mechanical thinking in combination with the program's presence in over 70 percent of American public schools takes too much power and judgment away from students and teachers. Instead of empowering both parties to exercise discretion, they are rewarded for compliance to an enormously wealthy centralized authority's increasingly schematic expectations. (2023, 126)

13. Many of my students came to school hungry.

14. As Tom Newkirk, editor of this book, once told me, "Standardized writing creates standardized thinkers."

Essays that drive mechanical thinking also drive mechanical reading. Many universities share this concern as well. Some offer no credit for AP. Others continue to give students college credit for passing AP English Literature and Composition, for example, but they are not giving them credit for freshman composition. These universities have recognized that students can pass the AP test without breaking free of the mechanical writing (and thinking) that the test values.[15] In 2023, more than 80 percent of four-year colleges did not require standardized tests like the SAT or ACT for admission (cited in Nietzel 2022). However, this trend may be changing. Recent evidence has found SAT scores to be a more accurate predictor of college success than a student's grades (Friedman, Sacerdote, and Tine 2024). As a result, more universities are bringing back the SAT into their admission criteria, which means even more emphasis in K–12 will be placed on mechanical thinking and writing.

CLOSING THOUGHTS

Our general ability to learn is highly correlated with general knowledge. The more you know about baseball, or music, or math, the more you are able to learn about baseball, or music, or math. In fact, the correlation between having general knowledge and learning was found to be *twice as high* as the correlation attributed to socioeconomic status (Lubinski and Humphreys 1997). Your ability to learn rests largely on what you already know, regardless of your background.

I was reminded of this yesterday when I met with a group of students who were reading Clint Smith's *How the Word Is Passed*, a thought-provoking tour of many of the nation's historical sites in which Smith probes the untold history of each place. The students, who were halfway through the book, were struggling. Through conferring with them, I realized that much of their confusion and disconnection was rooted in their lack of prior knowledge. Not only had the students never visited any of the sites, but they had never *heard* of them. This unfamiliarity not only made the reading much more difficult but also contributed to them questioning why they had to study any of these landmarks in the first place.[16] Alberto Manguel, author of *The History of Reading*, reminds us, "Everything proceeds in geometric progression based on what

15. And that is *a lot* of mechanical writing and thinking: In 2021, over 839,000 students took either the AP language or the AP literature exam (Miller 2022).

16. Having students read books that are completely unfamiliar to them is not necessarily a bad thing. But it is a hard thing. It requires careful front-loading (as discussed in the last chapter) and other means of support from the teacher, especially in a classroom of students who are largely unmotivated readers.

is known and what is remembered every time we read something new" (cited in Wolf 2019, 88). These students lacked the general historical knowledge that would have helped them make important connections. "Geometric progression" was not possible. It is difficult to think deeply about something you know nothing about.

Having knowledge not only helps you learn more but also fuels your curiosity. As Ian Leslie, author of *Curious*, notes, curiosity "is stimulated by understanding *and* by the absence of understanding" (2015, 36). If you know nothing about a subject—say neoclassical architecture, for example—you are unlikely to want to discuss it. But if you already know something about the topic at hand, you are much more likely to be curious. Leslie says, "The more we know about something, the more intense our curiosity is about what we *don't* know" (38). Curiosity is generated, he says, when we find ourselves in the "curiosity zone"—that place where we have some knowledge but not too much knowledge (38). Leslie rejects the notion that some students are more curious than others; instead, what really matters is the context in which students encounter new information. Not having any context creates indifference.

Students who know a lot learn more, and they are more likely to widen their curiosity, which also brings them to another benefit: they develop the ability to think at deeper levels. Consider those whom we consider experts. In *How People Learn*, the National Research Council notes that

> **experts, regardless of the field, always draw on a richly structured information base; they are not just "good thinkers" or "smart people." The ability to plan a task, to notice patterns, to generate reasonable arguments and explanations, and to draw analogies to other problems are also more closely intertwined with factual knowledge than what was once believed. (Bransford, Brown, and Cocking 2000, 14)**

Good thinkers have built a reservoir of knowledge. Tom Loveless, a senior fellow in the Governance Studies program at the Brookings Institution, echoes this notion: "One of the most highly replicated findings of education research is that a good predictor of *how much students will learn tomorrow is how much they know today*. Studies of interventions that simply ratchet up expectations without regard for students' prior knowledge have yielded disappointing results" (2021; italics mine).

There is a lot at stake here. Maryanne Wolf, expert in cognitive neurosciences, worries that we rely too much on external knowledge at the expense of not building internal knowledge. Doing so would affect our ability to think critically, leading us to "become increasingly susceptible human beings who are more and more easily led by sometimes dubious, sometimes even false information that we mistake for knowledge, or, worse, do not care one way or another" (2019, 55). When we don't own our knowledge, we are put in a precarious position wherein we are forced to rely on others to do our thinking for us.[17]

Building this internal knowledge is critical, and the earlier, the better. Daniel Willingham (2012) reminds us, "Once kids are fluent decoders, much of the difference among readers is not due to whether they're a 'good reader' or a 'bad reader' (meaning they have good or bad reading skills). Much of the difference among readers is due to how wide a range of knowledge they have." This bears repeating: much of the difference between "good" and "bad" readers is strongly correlated with the amount of knowledge they possess. It is important to teach students the moves good readers make, but we must not lose sight of the fact that these moves are contingent on the reader knowing things.[18]

☆–☆–☆

So what can teachers do to help students become knowers? Here are ten suggestions.

10 THINGS TEACHERS CAN DO TO BUILD PRIOR KNOWLEDGE IN STUDENTS

1. **Explain the importance of prior knowledge.**
   Most students do not understand the value of prior knowledge. Teach the importance early in the year. Start with political cartoons and memes in which they can read the words but don't have enough context to make sense of what they are reading. Work up to passages and articles. Explain to students that one cannot think deeply, or argue a serious point, without owning knowledge on the topic. Remind them that how much they will learn in the future will depend largely on how much they know.

17. Exhibit A: Since Wolf wrote that passage, we now live in a society where nearly one-third of Americans still wrongly believe that the results of the 2020 presidential election were fraudulent (Kamisar 2023).

18. Knowledgeable readers not only read better but are likely to develop the ability to read faster, as knowing things cuts down on the need to reread things that are unfamiliar (Willingham 2021).

2. **Teach students that confusion is normal, especially when you lack prior knowledge.**
   Confusion is often rooted in not knowing enough about the topic. Teach students to embrace confusion instead of being afraid of it. Confusion is an opportunity to learn, and the more you learn, the less confusing things become. Model how you work through your confusion when reading, and show students how you connect to prior knowledge to work through your confusion.

3. **Teach students the value of long reading.**
   Books uniquely provide readers with deeper knowledge (as opposed to passage study or click-and-go reading). Give students time to read in class, and as the year progresses, stretch that time out. Help them to develop a quiet eye. Make it a goal that students will be able to sit and read for an uninterrupted hour by the end of the school year—a far stretch for those students who begin the year suffering from distraction addiction. State this goal at the beginning of the year and work toward it.

4. **Balance the reading diet.**
   Move away from teaching only the classics. Find books that are tuned in to the students. Give them choices. In their study of four hundred students, Ivey and Johnston (2023) found that when students had choice and access to books they were interested in, their volume of reading took off and their reading achievement greatly improved. There is important knowledge to be gleaned from self-selected books. For example, when some of my students read *We Are Not from Here*—not a core work—they gained a lot of knowledge about the plight of refugees.

5. **Make volume a top priority.**
   It will not matter how many standards you teach if students are not reading. Make the elimination of fake reading a top priority. Remember, the more balanced the reading diet, the more likely students will read, and the more they read, the more knowledge they will acquire. Have students complete a log of books they've read (and abandoned). The number of books a student reads is a strong indicator of success throughout K–12 and beyond.

6. **Surround them with books they want to read.**
   Building a classroom library is a career-long project. I was still building mine in my thirty-fifth year. Yes, there is value in taking your students to the school library—and I hope you do—but there is also *power* in giving students

immediate daily access to good books in the classroom. Book readers build deeper knowledge. To make that happen, students need daily access to books that interest them. Conduct daily book talks to entice them.

7. **Give them time to read in school.**
   As my friend Penny Kittle says, "If students are not reading with you, they are not reading without you"—another reason to devote some class time to reading. In *180 Days* (Gallagher and Kittle 2018), we write about how we devoted the first ten minutes of every class period to in-class reading, and while students were reading, we conducted one-on-one reading conferences. This personal interaction with each student is the key to breaking the fake reading habit. Never lose sight of volume, volume, volume.

8. **Ditch the vocabulary quizzes, but teach word-attack skills.**
   Time spent on weekly vocabulary lists would be better spent by having students read. There is a value, however, in teaching students knowledge about how words are constructed. Teach them the common prefixes, roots, and suffixes. Model what you do when confronted with an unfamiliar word. Again, a volume of reading is critical to overcoming word poverty. Deeper thinking is very difficult when one's vocabulary is limited. Restricted knowledge of words restricts thinking and makes learning harder.

9. **Find the sweet spot of framing.**
   The most difficult novel to teach is often the one that is farthest away from the students' prior knowledge. Often the framing you do before students read plays a critical role in their comprehension and thus motivation. Constantly ask yourself key questions: *How much framing do they need? How much is not enough? How much is too much? Where's the tipping point between helping and enabling? What can I do to ensure students will keep reading?*

10. **Assign an article of the week regularly.**
    We are not literature teachers; we are literacy teachers. Choose weekly articles that will inform students (which is not the same as picking articles that will entertain them). Lure them out of their entertainment bubbles. Annotate an article in front of the students, modeling your thinking as you do so. Stop at least once a quarter and remind students why you are asking them to read these weekly articles (see tip 1 in this list). Revisit their importance when enthusiasm lags.

It occurs to me that keeping all ten of these tips in your head at all times may be a bit much. So let me conclude this book by further reducing the list. To do this, I am thinking of Michael Pollan's influential book *In Defense of Food*, where in the introduction he boils down the secret to a healthy diet in a succinct list:

> **Eat food. Not too much. Mostly plants. (2009, 1)**

With apologies to Pollan, I leave you with my imitation:

> To read stuff you have to know stuff.
>
> Knowing stuff is better than looking stuff up.
>
> One cannot think deeply without knowing a lot of stuff.

WORKS CITED

Abrams, Annie. 2023. *Shortchanged: How Advanced Placement Cheats Students*. Baltimore, MD: Johns Hopkins University Press.

Bransford, John D., Ann L. Brown, and Rodney R. Cocking, eds. 2000. *How People Learn: Brain, Mind, Experience, and School*. Expanded ed. With M. Suzanne Donovan, John D. Bransford, and James W. Pellegrino, eds. Washington, DC: National Academy Press. https://nap.nationalacademies.org/read/9853/chapter/1#ii.

Cineas, Fabiola. 2023. "The Controversy over AP African American Studies, Explained." Vox. Updated February 9. https://www.vox.com/policy-and-politics/23583240/ap-african-american-studies-college-board-florida-ron-desantis.

Dederer, Claire. 2023. *Monsters: A Fan's Dilemma*. New York: Alfred A. Knopf.

Dissinger, Matt, Shannon Furman, and Tim Rumpff, dirs. 2023. *Quarterback*. Aired July 12 on Netflix. https://www.netflix.com/title/81482895.

Friedman, John, Bruce Sacerdote, and Michele Tine. 2024. *Standardized Test Scores and Academic Performance at Ivy-Plus Colleges*. Opportunity Insights. http://opportunityinsights.org/wp-content/uploads/2024/01/SAT_ACT_on_Grades.pdf.

Gallagher, Kelly, and Penny Kittle. 2018. *180 Days: Two Teachers and the Quest to Engage and Empower Adolescents*. Portsmouth, NH: Heinemann.

Garcia, Antero, and Ernest Morrell. 2022. *Tuned-In Teaching: Centering Youth Culture for an Active and Just Classroom*. Portsmouth, NH: Heinemann.

Gruver, Mead. 2023. "Fired Librarians Who Opposed Book Bans Turn to Civil Rights Agency for Redress." *Los Angeles Times*, November 8. https://www.latimes.com/world-nation/story/2023-11-08/librarians-turn-to-civil-rights-agency-to-oppose-book-bans-and-their-firings.

Hirsch, E. D., Jr. 1988. *Cultural Literacy: What Every American Needs to Know.* New York: Vintage Books.

———. 2001. "Seeking Breadth and Depth in the Curriculum." *Educational Leadership* 59 (2): 22–25. https://www.ascd.org/el/articles/seeking-breadth-and-depth-in-the-curriculum.

Ivey, Gay, and Peter Johnston. 2023. "What Happens When Young People Actually Read 'Disturbing' Books." *Teachers College Press* (blog), October 31. https://www.tcpress.com/blog/young-people-read-disturbing-books/.

Kamisar, Ben. 2023. "Almost a Third of Americans Still Believe the 2020 Election Result Was Fraudulent." *Meet the Press* (blog), June 20. https://www.nbcnews.com/meet-the-press/meetthepressblog/almost-third-americans-still-believe-2020-election-result-was-fraudule-rcna90145.

Kittle, Penny, and Kelly Gallagher. 2022. *4 Essential Studies: Beliefs and Practices to Reclaim Student Agency.* Portsmouth, NH: Heinemann.

Leslie, Ian. 2015. *Curious: The Desire to Know and Why Your Future Depends on It.* New York: Basic Books.

Liu, Eric. 2015. "What Every American Should Know." *The Atlantic*, July 3. https://www.theatlantic.com/politics/archive/2015/07/what-every-american-should-know/397334/.

Loveless, Tom. 2021. "Why Common Core Failed." Brookings. March 18. https://www.brookings.edu/articles/why-common-core-failed/.

Lubinski, David, and Lloyd G. Humphreys. 1997. "Incorporating General Intelligence into Epidemiology and the Social Sciences." *Intelligence* 24 (1): 159–201. https://www.sciencedirect.com/science/article/abs/pii/S0160289697900167.

Marzano, Robert J. 2003. *What Works in Schools: Translating Research into Action.* Alexandria, VA: ASCD.

Marzano, Robert J., and John S. Kendall. 1998. *Awash in a Sea of Standards.* Technical report. Aurora, CO: Mid-continent Research for Education and Learning. https://cdnsm5-ss11.sharpschool.com/UserFiles/Servers/Server_61078/File/Academics/Curriculum/5982IR_AwashInASea.pdf.

Miller, Danika. 2022. "What Are the Most Popular AP Exams?" BestColleges.Com. www.bestcolleges.com/blog/most-popular-ap-exams/.

Mintz, Steven. 2022. "In Defense of Cultural Literacy." *Higher Ed Gamma* (blog), March 20. https://www.insidehighered.com/blogs/higher-ed-gamma/defense-cultural-literacy.

Nietzel, Michael T. 2022. "More than 80% of Four-Year Colleges Won't Require Standardized Tests for Fall 2023 Admissions." *Forbes*, November 15. https://www.forbes.com/sites/michaeltnietzel/2022/11/15/more-than-80-of-four-year-colleges-wont-require-standardized–tests-for-fall-2023-admissions/.

OECD. 2020. *Curriculum Overload: A Way Forward.* Paris: OECD Publishing. https://doi.org/10.1787/3081ceca-en.

Phelps, Richard. 2023. "Are English Departments Really Dying?" James G. Martin Center for Academic Renewal. May 10. https://www.jamesgmartin.center/2023/05/are-english-departments-really-dying/.

Pollan, Michael. 2009. *In Defense of Food: An Eater's Manifesto.* New York: Penguin Books.

Reeves, Douglas. 2021. "Power Standards." Douglas Reeves, March 23. YouTube video, 5:42. https://www.youtube.com/watch?v=Bf7s1BhrWrQ.

Rosenshine, Barak V. 2015. "How Time Is Spent in Elementary Classrooms." *Journal of Classroom Interaction* 50 (1): 41–53.

Schmoker, Mike. 2020. "Radical Reset: The Case for Minimalist Literacy Standards." *Educational Leadership* 77 (5): 44–50. https://www.ascd.org/el/articles/radical-reset-the-case-for-minimalist-literacy-standards.

Schmoker, Mike, and Robert J. Marzano. 1999. "Realizing the Promise of Standards-Based Education." *Educational Leadership* 56 (6): 17–21. https://www.ascd.org/el/articles/realizing-the-promise-of-standards-based-education.

Vander Ark, Tom. 2017. "What Is Curriculum? From Managed Instruction to Personalized Learning." *Education Week*, January 2. https://www.edweek.org/technology/opinion-what-is-curriculum-from-managed-instruction-to-personalized-learning/2017/01.

Walker, Tim. 2017. "The Secret to High-Performing Nations' Success? A Respected, Professionalized Teaching Force." *NEA News*. www.nea.org/nea-today/all-news-articles/secret-high-performing-nations-success-respected-professionalized-teaching-force.

Willingham, Daniel. 2012. "School Time, Knowledge, and Reading Comprehension." *Daniel Willingham: Science and Education* (blog), March 7. https://www.danielwillingham.com/daniel-willingham-science-and-education-blog/school-time-knowledge-and-reading-comprehension.

———. 2021. *Why Don't Students Like School? A Cognitive Scientist Answers Questions About How the Mind Works and What It Means for the Classroom*. San Francisco: Jossey-Bass.

Wilson, Leslie Owen. n.d. *Types of Curriculum.* EVA Education. https://evaeducation.weebly.com/uploads/1/9/6/9/19692577/1a._types_of_curriculum.pdf. Accessed October 10, 2023.

Wolf, Maryanne. 2019. *Reader, Come Home: The Reading Brain in a Digital World.* New York: Harper.

Index

C

D

I

J

K

L

M

N

O

Q

R

S